"A documentary is only as good as its subject. For *Levees*, we had an abundance of heroic and eloquent individuals—black, white, Hispanic, male, female, young, and old—who shared themselves with the world. As we made more trips down to New Orleans, it became apparent to me that Phyllis had emerged as the dominant voice in the piece. . . . I hope you too will discover what I did. Phyllis Montana-Leblanc is a fine writer, a true original American voice."

—Spike Lee

## Praise for Phyllis Montana-Leblanc

"The real 'stars' of [Spike Lee's documentary *When the Levees Broke*] are people—black and white. . . . Some are angry, like the irrepressibly eloquent Phyllis Montana-Leblanc."

—*San Francisco Chronicle*

"One of the rawest specimens of classic Nawlins spitfire you'll ever find . . . Leblanc is a frequently hilarious presence, a fuming Greek chorus of one."

—*Newsweek*

"One of the film's most impassioned voices. . . . She is alternately poetic and profane. And her influence throughout the film is haunting."

—*Austin American-Statesman*

# NOT JUST THE LEVEES BROKE

## MY STORY DURING AND AFTER HURRICANE KATRINA

### PHYLLIS MONTANA-LEBLANC

**ATRIA** PAPERBACK

New York   London   Toronto   Sydney

**ATRIA** PAPERBACK

A Division of Simon & Schuster, Inc.
1230 Avenue of the Americas
New York, NY 10020

First Atria Paperback edition August 2009

**ATRIA** PAPERBACK and colophon are
trademarks of Simon & Schuster, Inc.

For information about special discounts for bulk purchases,
please contact Simon & Schuster Special Sales at
1-866-506-1949 or business@simonandschuster.com.

The Simon & Schuster Speakers Bureau can bring authors
to your live event. For more information or to book an event
contact the Simon & Schuster Speakers Bureau at
1-866-248-3049 or visit our website at www.simonspeakers.com.

Designed by Suet Y. Chong

Manufactured in the United States of America

3   5   7   9   10   8   6   4   2

The Library of Congress has cataloged the hardcover edition as follows:
Montana-Leblanc, Phyllis.
Not just the levees broke: my story during and after Hurricane Katrina/
Phyllis Montana-Leblanc.—1st Atria Books hardcover ed.
   p.   cm.
1. Montana-Leblanc, Phyllis. 2. Montana-Leblanc, Phyllis——Family.
3. New Orleans (La.)—Biography. 4. African-American women—
Louisiana—New Orleans—Biography. 5. Disaster victims—Louisiana—
New Orleans—Biography. 6. Hurricane Katrina, 2005. 7. Hurricane Katrina,
2005—Social aspects— Louisiana—New Orleans. 8. New Orleans (La.)—
Social conditions—21st century. I. Title.

F379.N553M58 2008
363.34'9220976090511—dc22          2008022350

ISBN 978-1-4165-6347-1
ISBN 978-1-4165-6618-2 (ebook)

*I dedicate this book to my one and only true love:*
*Mr. Ron A. Leblanc Sr.*

*My love for you grows each time I breathe.*
*There is nothing that I wouldn't do for you,*
*and the music I love best is your laughter.*
*You loved me through the worst experience in my entire life*
*and I appreciate you.*

*Finally, I want to thank God for you because*
*only He could place two hearts such as ours together,*
*and I promise to be a better, stronger human being.*

*Will you marry me again on January 3, 2009?*
*Your wife for infinity,*
*Mrs. Phyllis Montana-Leblanc.*

"The most important thing to remember about the drowning of New Orleans is that it wasn't a natural disaster."

—Michael Grunwald,
*Newsweek,*
August 13, 2007

# SPIRITS WON'T BE BROKEN

Our film crew flew into the Louis Armstrong International Airport in New Orleans, Louisiana, the day after Thanksgiving. The very first person to be interviewed for my documentary *When the Levees Broke* was Phyllis Montana-Leblanc. We were cordial to each other upon introduction. I remember that before we started filming she asked me quietly if it was OK for her to curse. I quickly reassured her that it was. I wanted Phyllis to be honest in her thoughts, to be comfortable in front of the camera, and if she needed to be profane, *so be it*. I was amazed. Phyllis was not just cursing to be cursing; somehow her observations were not profane but profound. She spoke with passion and intelligence about the near-death experience of surviving the debacle of Hurricane Katrina.

A documentary is only as good as its subjects. For *Levees*, we had an abundance of heroic and eloquent individuals—black, white, Hispanic, male, female, young, and old—who shared themselves with the world. As we made more trips down to New Orleans, it became apparent to me that Phyllis had emerged as the dominant voice in the piece.

On our final trip, we filmed Phyllis in her FEMA trailer where she gave me a big surprise. She asked me if she could read on camera a poem she had written the night before. To be honest I have never been a fan of poetry and was not expecting much. But being cordial I said, go ahead and read it. We rolled the camera and in painful and truthful words she summed up the entire four-hour documentary. Silently I thought, "Thank God. Now we have an ending."

I hope you too will discover what I did. Phyllis Montana-Leblanc is a fine writer, a true Original American Voice.

As I write this foreword, she still lives in her FEMA trailer with her husband, Ron, and their Yorkshire terrier, Brooklyn (*great name*). She struggles with the rest of her be-leaguered city. People trying to get back on track. Let's all pray for her and New Orleans.

—Spike Lee

NOT JUST THE
LEVEES
BROKE

Thursday, August 25, 2005

Tropical Storm Katrina becomes a Category One
hurricane, hitting South Florida.

**1** My husband and I start hearing about the hurricane and the chances of it hitting New Orleans on August 26, 2005. I call my sister Catherine and we decide that my husband, Ron, and I will go over to her house and bring her and her son Nicholas over to my mom's apartment so that we can be together. Catherine lived about a mile away from us in eastern New Orleans. Ironically, that's where our FEMA trailer is now located.

Mom's apartment was directly across from ours. She had moved there after a short stay with my sister Cheryl in Los Angeles. When Ron and I first walk out of the apartment, I look up at the sky. I notice an odd kind of gray color, but otherwise it's a normal day. I pause for a second in thought and then go about the business of getting my family.

I'm looking around as Ron is driving and I'm thinking,

"What in the fuck is about to happen to us and this city?" I think this because the newscasters are saying that a huge storm could possibly happen but "it's not definite at this time."

This is why we're so confused and don't know whether to run for our lives or just "ride it out." We've had this happen before where the weather people tell us that the forecast is bad and then that turns out not to be the case. We are cautious kind of by nature, and wait to see what's up. But, honestly, this time I have a feeling that something is about to go down in a serious-ass way. We get to Catherine's home and start packing her truck.

My nephew Nicholas is running around without a care in the world. I envy him right about now. He has autism and is unaware of "real time." I know it sounds crazy, but in anxious moments like this, you do what you have to do to mentally escape.

So, we're packing juices, clothes, Nicholas's backpacks that Catherine has just purchased for school, cans of food, extra bottles of water, Nicholas's school uniforms, and her favorite music that her late husband had taped for her. And just as we're ready to head back to our apartment complex, Catherine yells that she has to go back in the house to get her husband's pictures. All I can say to Ron is "Oh, my God, not now." She runs into the house and grabs the picture of their wedding and jumps into her truck. Her husband, Helmon Michael Gordon Jr., succumbed to liver cancer on September 4, 2004.

We ride back to the complex and all the time I'm thinking that all of this effort is for nothing. Ain't no damn hurricane gon' hit New Orleans, this is some bullshit! Every time they tell us there's a hurricane, people begin running for their lives and nothing happens. So we get to my mom's apartment. Once we situate Catherine and Nicholas, Ron and I go back to our place. I put the Weather Channel on and begin to cook and put food away in ziplock bags. The media are saying we need food for the two or three days when we may be without power.

I know people say that black folks love some chicken and I gotta say they are correct. I fry chicken, barbecue chicken, smother chicken, buffalo-wing some chicken. You name it, I did it to the chicken, okay? I fixed some egg and rice for Nicholas and some gravy and rice, because those are his favorite foods. I fill our tub up with water because the news is saying to "fill your tubs up with water, just in case you need to flush your toilets." Then I remember something that I used to see my mother do back in the '70s when there was a predicted hurricane. I put gray electrical tape on all of our windows so that if the wind breaks the windows, they won't shatter and cut anyone.

All the time I'm running around doing all of this, Ron is looking at me and not saying anything because he would upset me. Ron later told me that the way I was yelling and screaming he was thinking that I was going to have a mental breakdown or a heart attack. He'd already made up his mind to let me do what I wanted and that's why he only called my name every few minutes or so in hopes I'd calm down. I have to do what I have to do, and nothing is going to stop me. My anxiety is building by the minute because the media's starting to talk about what to do if water comes into your home and you have to go into your attic. They are recommending that we keep handy a hammer or something that could make a hole through the ceiling to your rooftop. I was like, "Oh, hell no, fuck this, this shit is about to be serious."

So, I begin to think, if it's going to be this serious, why in the hell is there no mandatory evacuation right now? What does the mayor have to say about that? Where is the governor? Why are they not telling us to get the hell out of town? So, I'm thinking maybe, just maybe, this is all for nothing. Don't worry, Phyllis, this is all going to pass us by just like it always does. Still, I prepare. Just in case.

Friday, August 26

Governor Katherine Blanco declares a state of
emergency in the State of Louisiana, as Katrina is
upgraded to Category Two and has passed into the
Gulf of Mexico.

Saturday, August 27

Katrina is upgraded to Category Three. Mayor
Ray Nagin calls for a voluntary evacuation of New
Orleans. President Bush declares a federal state of
emergency for Louisiana and gives FEMA authority
to provide aid.

The night of Saturday, August 27, 2005, we sleep and all is well. But the weather forecasters are still watching the storm. She's not in the Gulf and as long as she doesn't come there, we're okay. We wake up on Sunday, August 28, 2005, and the news is now saying that Hurricane Katrina is in the "Gulf" and predicted to hit New Orleans.

Okay, I fry more chicken and call Catherine and tell her what I just saw on the news. "Do you see how big this bitch is?" I ask and then say, "We got to get the fuck out of here." Catherine says, "I'm ready, 'cause you know if Mike was here we wouldn't even be here right now. We'd be gone to Texas by now." My mom is in the background saying that she's not leaving. She says that her legs are hurting and nothing's probably going to happen anyway.

"You know what, if Momma wants to stay, then let her.

She's got her neighbors if she needs anything," I say to Catherine, laughing the entire time because we both know we aren't leaving our momma. But I'm starting to get worried with all this damn talk about "keep a hammer just in case you have to bust a hole in your attic to come out on the roof" and "fill your tub up so you can flush the damn toilet." It's as if all of these people know what the hell is going to happen and they aren't telling us the real deal, you know? Then Catherine adds to my damn worry by telling me that she forgot something at her house and needs to go back. We jump in her truck and ride back to her house.

We notice fewer and fewer cars on the street, and people gone. The sky looks weird. The clouds are dark gray, light gray, white, and almost black. And they aren't all together at this point in time. They're all separated, as if they know that once they connect all hell will break loose. Looking at them, they seem to go through my eyes and down into my soul. There is the most horrible feeling of fear, and at the same time I feel a strange beauty in it. What come to my mind are two words: *ominous* and *ethereal*. It reminds me of a really handsome man who is gorgeous to look at but evil behind his face. As much as I enjoy looking at it, I feel something bad behind it, like this is going to be really, really bad—like the end of the world or something. Street after street is empty. The stores are closed and houses boarded up and there is silence in the city. The only thing we need now is for tumbleweed to roll across the street and that would do me in, for real.

So we get to Catherine's house and I'm telling her to hurry up because it's starting to rain. It's only a couple of sprinkles but my anxiety and panic are starting to grow. We should grab what she came for and get the hell back to the apartment complex. I stop rushing her when I see that she's come back to get more of Michael's photos. Some are of him in college—he attended Southern University in Baton Rouge, Louisiana, and was a member of Kappa Kappa Psi fraternity. She grabs Nicholas's one-piece life jacket just in case the waters overwhelm us, so the rising waters won't pull him away. Her worst fear is Nicholas drowning and that's why she is so frantic about getting his life jacket, which is really what she used when they went swimming. We take Michael's pictures and a few toys for Nicholas, and these paper flowers that Michael had made for her out of construction paper with his own hands as his life was being completely consumed by the cancer.

On the ride back we see police cars riding up and down the streets, patrolling the neighborhoods . . . probably for looters. There was lots of talk later about how shocking it is when people steal during a bad time. But a criminal isn't going to change his or her behavior because everybody is in a bad situation. It's just a fact of life. We get back and I look across the street to a neighboring apartment complex, Pirogue Cove, and it's practically empty: from what I can see, only a few people around. We walk up the stairs and Catherine goes over to my mom's apartment and I return to ours, where Ron is waiting for me.

I double-check again to make sure that the apartment is in order and listen to the weather reports. We are now in the path of Hurricane Katrina. And, at about nineteen hours before Katrina is predicted to hit New Orleans, the mayor of

New Orleans, C. Ray Nagin, announces a mandatory evacuation. Nineteen hours! What in the hell took our city's officials so long to place this order?

I call Catherine and ask her if she's seen the same thing on the news and she says yes. Now I'm in panic mode and yelling that we should leave, and leave right now. I hear the weatherman say that if you haven't left by now it's best to hunker down and just get ready to "ride it out." He keeps repeating what tools to have on hand just in case you have to go through your ceiling and come out on top of your roof, and that shit is freaking me out more by the second. My heart is racing a hundred miles a minute and I keep telling myself that it won't be that bad. I keep thinking that they are exaggerating this storm, but my heart is filled to the top with fear. I have been through different storms in my life and this is the first time I actually think I might not survive it.

Ron, in the meantime, is asking me to calm down. He says that everything's going to be okay. I swear, I want to cuss him out and just start walking up the street; that's how out of control my thinking started to get. But I know better, and decide to try to collect my thoughts. That lasts a good five minutes, and I'm back to checking the windows to make sure the tape is in place.

I walk around our apartment complex and see that there are quite a few people still there, and this helps to calm me down. Then I think, oh, God, that's how many bodies will be floating when this is all over. Okay, come back, Phyllis. I have got to get myself together, I think. When I walk over to my mother's apartment, they are sitting down watching television and we talk a little while about what could possibly happen. My mother, Rita, is being very positive about nothing ever happening and this will all pass us by. I leave and walk out to the parking lot, looking at the sky again, and I gotta tell you, you can feel the bad. I'm dead serious. This is the worst feeling I've had in my life.

I go back upstairs by Ron and of course he's telling me the same old shit about relaxing and calming down. The news is scaring the living shit out of me, so Mr. Ron suggests that we turn the television off for a while. Oh, yeah, that will work out just great. Turn off the television and let my imagination just take over and kill me right there on the spot. Needless to say, Ron decides to leave the television on to help his wife calm down. Great idea! Fuck! I don't know if anyone who's never experienced this before can imagine sitting and waiting for disaster to strike and not knowing if today is your last day alive. The pressure on my heart is so intense that I want to just crawl inside of a closet with earplugs and a blanket, close my eyes, and make it all just go away. I start singing in my mind, "Rain, rain, go away, come again another day." Now, do you think that works? I'm trying to find a way to not lose my mind. I have four sisters and a brother—Gina, Catherine, Cheryl, Lisa, and Thomas—and I've always wondered which one of us would end up being "the crazy one."

I choose to hang on to who I am: a strong black woman. I begin to think of all of the bad things I've been through in my life and how I overcame them. For example, when I was a teenager and this "boyfriend" decided that I was his punching bag. I was only a teenager and for five years he physically, sexually, verbally, and mentally abused me, and not that someone needs a reason—because there is no reason for someone to do this to another human being—but he had no reason to hurt me that badly to the point where I just wanted to die to get away from it all. I did try to commit suicide, but God wanted me here for a reason. I have come a long way and if I survived those other "storms," I can do this. Y'all, there is nothing worse than knowing that you are in a fight for your actual life and not know if you will lose.

The news is still saying that it's now too late to leave. They're also saying that we'll only be without power for about three to four days. Okay, not too bad. Maybe we're going to be okay. A little smelly and hungry, but okay. Catherine, my mom, and me talk back and forth and every few minutes I walk over to where they're talking with the neighbors and laughing about how all those fools are running for nothing and people will be stealing everything not nailed down. We eat and bathe so at least to have a head start on what is predicted to come. I forget about looking at the sky. It's as if we all are feeding off each other's strengths and weaknesses. You know, like real life. As evening begins to fall upon us things start to quiet down and then you can feel the "get ready" in the air—although no one says those exact words. My family members and I keep our cell phones plugged into the wall when we talk on them so we have a full charge when the power goes out. Then darkness comes. We still have electricity. Even as I'm writing this, my heart is starting to beat a little faster because I already know what's going to happen next and I want to cry. I want to scream. I want to never remember what happens next. Ron and I are in our apartment and my mom, sister, and nephew are across the way from us and we are all watching the news and calling each other back and forth. Ron then decides to move our bed alongside the wall. I think that's a little uncool. But it seems like a good idea at the time to him and gives me something else to think about.

I do another run-through. I have the comforters nailed over the windows to block any breaking glass and that's a wrap for the day. Ron goes to lie down and soon falls asleep but I keep waking him to have someone to talk to to get the nervousness out of my system. He wakes up and talks to me and then falls asleep. I keep at it for a while and then give up, feeling sorry for him because he is very tired. I start praying. I ask God to please let us survive this storm and to not let us be killed by it.

I had met so many rotten men in my life. Ron was the best thing to ever come into my life and I want more: many, many more years with him. I think about losing him and what would happen if I lost my mother, sister, and nephew, and that just about wipes me out emotionally. I think I actually started growing gray hairs all in that one evening.

What does help is thinking about growing up in New Orleans. We used to have these sweet summer treats called Huckabucks—they were some type of frozen juice or Kool-Aid and people would sell them during the summertime. We would buy them from the homes of neighborhood women who were elderly and knew how to make them the right way. Our favorite house to go to was Ms. Hazel's because she put fruit cocktail in the bottom of her cups so you got more for your quarter. Sometimes you could buy them during winter season, but that was only from the desperate households, so we would just wait to go to Ms. Hazel's or another house if some kid found a better spot to go to. I start missing them. I wish that I had one because when you ate one it made you happy and all you thought about when you had one was that Huckabuck. Sometimes we'd call them Zips or Frozen Cups, and I just wanted something to make me happy and stop the fear.

I call Catherine, who is channel surfing, watching some BET awards show and the weather. Now it was definite: the news is saying New Orleans is in the direct path of Hurricane Katrina and we will be getting hit, and hard. Mayor C. Ray Nagin is saying that the director of weather is saying this is going to be the worst storm to hit the Gulf Coast in the history of this country.

Sunday, August 28

Mayor Nagin calls for a mandatory evacuation of New Orleans. Buses, trains, and most airlines have suspended service to and from the area. Katrina is declared a Category Five storm, the highest rating.

# 3

Why didn't anyone warn us sooner? Why didn't they (city, state, and all government officials) warn us of how bad this storm really was going to be?

My mind is filled with a million thoughts and each one of them is in the area of saying good-bye. I'm saying good-bye to my life as I have known it and forgetting about the future. I haven't even completed sharing my love with those I had yet to meet. I have so much love to give—Barry White's song was Ron's and my wedding song. We'd only been married for one year! What kind of shit is this? I was going to have a baby and Ron, his kids, and me were going to be one big family and have a big yard and grow together and make up for lost time. I'm wearing myself out mentally and soon decide to lie down and try to get some sleep. I don't think anymore about the trouble that is coming. I clear my mind to nothing. Blank.

No more past. No more future. Just lie down and go to sleep. God will take care and no matter what I pray for or want or wish, His Will Would Be Done.

I am thinking frantically about what to do next and I can't bring myself to any conclusions. I am out of ideas. I stand over my husband as he sleeps and softly kiss his forehead and then his lips. He moves around for a minute, but stays asleep. I just stand there looking at him in the candlelit room and think of how much I truly love this man. The last thing I do is put my fingers through his fingers and feel his love for me and transfer my love for him in the holding of his hand, praying that he can feel my love in his sleep.

I lie down next to him but I can't get comfortable. I walk to the living room and take some cushions off the sofa and lay them down on the floor alongside our bed. Still, I can't get comfortable. I go back on the bed. I go back on the floor. I crawl on the floor to the closet, then back on the bed. I can't tell you where I fell asleep. I can only tell you when I knew that we were in trouble: serious trouble.

August 29, 2005. Hurricane Katrina is just beginning to flick her tongue at the city I have called home my entire life: New Orleans, Louisiana. In the early morning hours I can hear the swooshing sounds and fear runs down my back. This is when I first realize trouble has officially arrived. We lose electricity and the winds begin to blow. My heart is racing and beating so hard that I can feel my chest jumping against my shirt. Ron lies on the bed, dozing off as I try frantically to find a safe place for us to hide. First I try putting pillows and blankets in our bedroom closet. That's too small and it's hard to breathe in there. Then I run to the living room and pull the leather cushions from the sofa and place them on the floor next to our bed. Finally, exhausted, I fall asleep, only to be awakened by the frightening sound of dripping water. It's so loud that it wakes me up and I start shaking Ron.

"Ron, wake up," I yell. "Wake up." I ask him to listen to find out where the sound of pouring water is coming from. We begin searching frantically to find it and then we look up. Water is pouring through the light fixture in the ceiling. Forgetting that the electricity is gone, I begin yelling at Ron that we're going to be electrocuted and the apartment is going to catch fire. I don't think at the moment about why or how the water is coming through. But we are soon to find out that the rooftops of the two apartments above us were blown off by the storm.

We can see that daylight is beginning to show through the corners of the window but we can't see out because of the blankets covering them. The wind gets stronger and stronger, louder and louder. It sounds like a train of water is passing over the apartment, right on top of us. We can hear the building being ripped apart as if by some big-ass woman. I don't know if you have ever seen this movie with Daryl Hannah called *Attack of the 50 Ft. Woman*. Well, that's what Katrina was, peeling our shit apart. Metal is crashing against the walls. Glass is breaking everywhere around us. As I run to the front of the apartment, I notice these swelling bubbles in the walls. "What in the hell are bubbles doing in the walls?" I ask myself. I can't understand what is happening. When I tell Ron to look at the walls the bubbles are all over. The water is coming in through the rooftop or our ceilings and is filling up the insides of the walls. Ron says, "The walls are breathing in and out." He says he can actually feel it against his leg. I yell that the apartment is flooding and we need to get out. Ron tries to calm me down, but it is not working. I want to get the fuck out of there. But go where? Out into the storm that is sure to be the death of us? Inside is death. Outside is death.

Our apartment is a one-bedroom that includes a living room, dining room, kitchen, bathroom, and bedroom. We're standing in the living room, my hand is on the doorknob but I will not, cannot open it. I'm crazy, literally crazy with fear. I'm blank. Then, *crash*! We hear the breaking and splitting of wood, and the rushing of water. Our bedroom ceiling has come falling down on top of the bed where Ron had lain only a few hours ago. The apartments above us are coming down on top of us. I'm screaming at the top of my lungs "Get me out of here! I don't want to die! Not like this!" *Crash* and *boom* again! The bathroom ceiling falls into the tub and toilet. Holding on to the back of Ron's shirt I decide we have to leave. I remember not being able to let go of Ron's shirt. We have to go out into Katrina's winds, and we don't know how many miles per hour they are blowing, or we will die in our apartment, buried under the rooftops of two levels of apartments above us.

I have to find my cell phone and call Catherine to find out if she can see outside. I need to tell her we have to get out because the ceilings are falling down around us. We have to get out. We just have to. The winds and the rain are whipping through the complex so hard that you cannot see outside. Each time I try the calls drop. Then I'm finally able to reach Catherine on her cell phone. I yell for her to look outside and see why everything is falling. She takes too long to answer, so I open the door. Then she yells into the phone for us to stay put because there is a two-by-four flying past our door! We slam the door shut. Oh, shit! How in the hell are we going to get out of here? We're trapped! Our phones go dead. I try to call Catherine again; I dialed so many times my fingers cramped.

Eventually, we get connected again. She tells us that the coast is clear, nothing is flying around. Ron cracks open the door enough to see for himself. It's not like we don't believe Catherine, but who are we kidding, in my fear I don't trust anyone. Not even myself. The entire time I'm holding on to the bottom part of Ron's shirt. I am not letting go. We have to stay together.

Now, why we come up with this next move I don't know. But this is our choice, or rather it's Ron's. The plan is to run down a flight of stairs to get into my mother-in-law's apartment in the same apartment complex. She lives with her daughter Valgean and her two young children. They had already evacuated out to Gramercy, Louisiana, where my other sister-in-law, Laurie, and her family are living. That area is in a safety zone, or at least more safe than New Orleans. We don't think we can chance running across to my mom's apartment because the space is too wide open. We don't want to take a chance on flying debris that could kill us. I say to Ron, "Once we go out this door, do not look back! I will be right behind you—just don't stop once we go out this door." Each time Ron cracks open the door, I slam it back shut. The fear of what is out there is too much. Once the door opens the wind from Hurricane Katrina takes my breath away. The rainwater stings my eyes, face, and arms. But I run. I run like I have stolen a pack of Now and Later candy and the store owner is chasing me. Then I hear the sounds of glass breaking, rooftops being ripped apart, the rain, the wind. My mind begins breaking apart slowly. I'm running for my life. We are running for our lives. I scream the entire time. No particular words come out. Just screams. It takes us just a few minutes to get to the downstairs apartment but it feels like hours.

Once we reach the bottom of the stairs of the first floor I am relieved to see that there is no water on the ground outside. The waters from the broken levees haven't reached us just yet. I think we've made it. We are still alive and we are going to make it! Thank you Jesus! We get into the downstairs apartment and I begin to assess the area. I go about telling Ron to hurry up and cover the front window first because that is our most vulnerable spot.

There is a recliner chair in the living room, and Ron sits in it as soon as we come in! I yell "Why are you sitting down!" There's no time to sit down! He just looks at me and he sits. Poor soul. I've worn him out. He just sits there. So I open the hall closet to see if I can climb in for cover but there is too much stuff piled in it. I go to the bathroom to see about putting blankets and comforters in the tub, but then think that if the damn ceiling comes down I'll be crushed. Okay, back to the living room. I start yelling at Ron to put up a comforter. No, a mattress up against the window is better, in case something comes flying through. Where the window is situated, if you were to stand directly in front of it you could see all the way down to the parking lot on the other side of the apartment complex. At the end of this are three concrete studs to stop people from parking on the grass. I'm afraid that the winds will pull them up and fly them through this window. He finally gets up and goes into his mother's bedroom and gets a mattress off her bed and puts it up against the front window. Okay, that's better. In the meantime, I'm in his sister Valgean's room putting her mattress up against her window. I mean that wind is blowing so damn hard I don't think I can hear. I know that doesn't make any sense but that's what's happening to me. I am deaf from fear.

Then it happens. A lightbulb in the kitchen ceiling explodes. Oh, my God! I jump up to see where the noise has come from and we see water coming through the light fixture. It's like reliving being in our upstairs apartment. I become more crazed thinking that the ceiling is now about to come down because water is coming through. And this is even worse because we are now on the bottom with two apartments on top of us. So if anything falls we'll get all of it on top of us. I'm begging Ron not to sit in the recliner chair. So he sits in another chair. I'm like, okay, that's going to make me feel better. So I pull the chair into the hallway between the closet, bathroom, and bedroom. That way, we have walls surrounding us in case something blows through one of the windows.

At this time we have no electricity. I call my sister Cheryl in California for her to see where the hurricane is. She can't call me but I could call her because the signal to reach us is gone. I tell her what our situation is. Then I tell her to check the Weather Channel and see how far off Katrina is. She's like, okay. I don't know, maybe it's me but she seems to be moving too damn slow. Trust me, it's me. You have someone on the phone yelling and screaming, and it will make their response seem slower, but it's really not. So she gets the channel and she said, "Phyllis, it's thirty minutes away." We hang up. I start praying. I call her again, then she tells me, "Phyllis, it's fifteen minutes away, but she's moving at ten to fifteen miles an hour, really slow." Then I call her back and she tells me, "Phyllis, it's right over y'all." I say, "Cheryl, I'm scared," and the line goes dead. I fall to my knees and begin to pray. I'm asking God to forgive me for all of my sins. I'm pleading for death to not come to us. Especially not to my husband. I do not want Ron to die. But hell, I don't want to die either. For some reason when you're with someone else, at least for me, you care more about them than yourself in that moment. Still can't figure it out. But I'm okay with it, and also he is such a beautiful soul and deserves to live. I, on the other hand, have been through some rough times and have done wrong things in life. All that matters now is for me to know that God forgives me, and He does.

I continue to pray. I mean I'm praying so fast that it sounds like I'm speaking Spanish. Not the language, but the speed. Because, you see, I can hear every word that I'm saying, just in a really fast way. I tell Ron that he should also ask forgiveness for any sins. I tell him I'll say the prayer and you just say Amen. I do and he does. I continue to pray and beg God for a way out alive, not knowing we have already received His mercy. Then we can hear the water. It's like waves of water blowing in the wind. "Oh, Lord Jesus! What is that?" I am really losing control over my mind. I can't think straight. I look up at Ron from on my knees behind the chair that he is sitting in and say, "You know what, Ron? You know what I never thought of? What if this is God's will? For us to die like this, right here, right now?" I never thought of that until just now. "Baaaaaby," Ron turns around, looks at me, and yells: "WE ARE NOT GOING TO DIE! I HAVE A PRAYING WIFE!"

I'd had no idea that he had been paying attention to all the times I used to sit in our bed doing my Bible study. Then something lifts me up. I can't tell you that it is my doing. It's something under my arms and legs that lifts me to a standing position. I can feel something in my heart and it feels really, really good and happy.

So I think about when you watch movies or television shows and people either joke about or are serious about seeing a "light" when you are about to die, so I start saying it to keep my sanity, because it would always seem unreal to me when I heard other people say it, so I just start saying, "Don't go into the light, Phyllis, don't go into the light." No, this is good and it is joyful. It is strong too. I stand up and then I hear somebody yelling: "Who-dee-whooo, who-dee-whooo." I'm like, okay. Now I know I'm losing my damn mind. Those words are from a rap song by somebody and I don't know who, but I hate that song! So here I am now hearing this. I must have died and gone to hell.

I asked Ron, "Do you hear that?" Wait. Stop. Listen. Do you hear that? Ron says, "Yeah, I hear it." He moves to open the front door. I freak out and push the door back closed.

I'm afraid that something will fly at us and hit Ron. If that would have happened I would have just lain right next to him and died with him. I could not have handled something happening to him. This is the honest-to-God truth. So Ron calms me down and says, "Phyllis, I have to open the door." I hold on to the back of his shirt and jeans while he cracks the door open. I know Ron must have wanted to just knock my ass out just to shut me up, but it's my sister Catherine calling to us to come to where they are on the other side of the apartment complex. Some other people are stranded in the complex as well. They're at the bottom of the stairway on the other side of the complex where my mom lives. Come on! They keep yelling for us to run over to their side. By now, I think the winds are at about 135 mph. I tell Ron the same as before when we were upstairs. When we leave out, just keep running and don't look back, but look for flying objects. We get ready. Ruuuuun! We go out the door.

Now this is different from upstairs because we are now on open ground. Anything can take us out as we travel between my mother-in-law's apartment and my mom's apartment. The water is about three feet high when we run across it, but the strong winds made it seem higher. I'm high-stepping like I'm in a second-line dance on Super Sunday. Man, I'm stepping. Ron too. I know my brother-in-law Helmon Michael Gordon Jr. is looking down from heaven proudly. Michael, Catherine's husband, was the first African-American drum major at John Ehret High School here in New Orleans. And that's how I'm stepping, just like Mike, a drum major for life. We get across and run up the stairs. Relief. That's the first time I feel relief. Real relief. Seeing others: my sister Catherine, my nephew Nicholas, my momma, Rita, and her neighbors. People that we know. Familiar faces. Well, that relief passes real damn quick! I thought we've gotten to a safe place but it's just a repeat of where Ron and me had come from. I mean, the good thing is that my family is okay, but it's no better. We get to a neighbor's apartment to find eleven people there. We go into the apartment and there's a battery-operated television, but you can barely hear it because everybody is talking. "Everybody!" I say to myself. "How can we know what's going on if we can't hear it?" But I keep quiet. I have no more fight left in me.

The other children in the apartment don't take too well to my nephew, Nicholas, who is in a pull-up diaper, running around doing his normal thing. They don't understand the way he expresses excitement or the way he interacts in general. I keep a close eye on him, trying to play with him myself to keep him busy. A good thing about his autism (if there could be a good thing) is that he is not completely aware of the present danger.

The adults engage in a lot of prayer and conversations to keep our sanity. Eventually we will have to leave this place and take individual charge of our own survival. I begin to wonder why me, my mom, and Nicholas are not at my mom's apartment with Catherine and Ron. I take Nicholas with me. My "own world" removes me emotionally from reality. It's an escape to a mental comfort zone until I feel strong enough to handle severe emotional stress. Here we are on the second floor of our apartment complex with five feet of water standing under us, with no electricity, running out of food, water, and everything to survive, and my mind and spirit are beginning to drift away from me, so I have to find a way to handle what's happening to us. Then I notice that some other people seem to not let our situation bother them as much. I mean, what is there to laugh about? Understanding that everybody takes things in a different way, I soon go into my own world. I feel a sense of defeat, survival, death, life, love, anger, and pure fucking disgust. How in the world does a day like this become a fucking cookout? Ron has decided that he would walk from my mom's apartment, in that filthy-ass poisoned water, and go into our apartment to see if he can find our barbecue grill so we can warm our food. Some people who none of us really know come over to the side of the complex where my mom's apartment and her neighbors are and they're laughing and joking and carrying on like the day was a cookout and we were not in serious trouble. It just seems too much like a party instead of a life-and-death situation and it bothers me mentally and I'm becoming angrier by the second. They soon go away and end up fighting during the night.

I am not in the mood to laugh and say, okay, just another day. Hell no! Then the damn wind gusts begin to come. This is after the storm had passed over us and the weather man was saying that it was a normal thing to feel these bursts of strong winds that would last for about five minutes but it seemed like longer because the fear of the storm is still in my mind. I'm tired. Kind of like I am right now, reliving this shit all over again. My mom is in the kitchen heating—or trying to heat—some gumbo for Nicholas using a candle. A candle! That is the true love of a grandmother, I tell you. In normal times, he visits Maw-maw, gets to eat all the junk he likes, watches TV. And then Catherine comes and picks him up. But not this time. This time there are no sweet treats. There is no warm food. There is no cold juice to help us bear the unmerciful heat.

Catherine, who has Crohn's disease, is going into what is called a "flare-up." Crohn's disease is an intestinal disorder. When a "flare-up" happens, she begins having severe diarrhea and vomiting. She becomes dehydrated quickly and can die. She's getting upset because she has to keep using the bathroom and I'm upset that she's upset. The only way we can flush the toilet is if I go with a bucket and get some of the water that is rising up the steps and fill up the back of the toilet. So, there I go, up, down, up, down. This is actually helping me because I get to focus on something other than the possibility of us dying. My mind is still racing, though. I'm still wondering if we'll be able to get out of here. I'm thinking about how much this feels like a "hostage situation." It's like we're being held hostage in our own apartment complex, in a city where I've lived all of my life and my country's emergency management system is not coming to help us.

My mom is still trying desperately to find a way to warm food for Nicholas because that candle didn't work. In the meantime, I'm trying to find something to lower my heart rate. I feel like my heart is going to explode. I try deep breathing. That doesn't work. Of course I'm praying but that only increases my panic. I think we're going to drown or starve to death. The winds start to blow again. I jump up and ask somebody, did they hear that? Nobody heard it. So I run from person to person asking them to listen to the wind. Then I hear glass breaking. I cannot believe that God is letting us be tortured like this. Why won't He just kill us? Just let us go and die? Why are we being treated like this? But, God isn't doing this to me. I am.

Monday, August 29

Governor Blanco asks the President for "everything you've got." Thirty-five hundred national guard troops help New Orleans's fifteen hundred police officers with rescue operations.

**4** Day two after the hurricane, early that morning.

The sound of glass breaking was caused by people breaking into unoccupied apartments. Maybe it was for survival, maybe for personal reasons. This was not important to me then and is not now. In my mother's apartment I begin to check for damages, leaks, and so forth. There are water stains in the ceiling and dripping water. Standing on the balcony of her second-floor apartment I notice that a rooftop from a different building has blown on top of the laundry room. What I didn't know at the time was that it came from the third-floor apartment above my mom's. When I did, after I looked above the roof, I panicked. As darkness falls so does my spirit. It's completely dark and I can hear every single sound in the night. People are in the distance drinking and laughing. There is window glass breaking, people running. The heat is unbearable. I mean it gets so bad that my sister Catherine is like, "Fuck this, I have to take this shirt off. Ron's my brother-in-law and he's asleep anyway." Ron is suffering so bad that me and Catherine spent all night fanning him with newspapers and whatever we can find. Catherine keeps saying to open the front window so if some air did blow we could feel it. I said no because I'm afraid that someone will break in and rape or hurt us. So we sleep with the front windows closed. It must be ninety degrees outside. I cannot sleep. I'm so afraid of what someone might do to us that I cannot sleep. My heart rate is still through the roof, and I'm afraid of having a heart attack. I try searching for something with a sedative in it that could make me go to sleep but can't find anything. Finally I find NyQuil capsules and take them. I sleep for a couple of hours and my heart rate goes down. But as soon as I wake up, so does my heart rate. I keep hearing helicopters fly by, and each time I do I run to the front door and start waving the flashlight, but no one sees me. It's too dark and I'm being a jackass. Then I hear them flying over the back of the apartment and I run to the back window and flash the flashlight, but still they do not see me. That's when I start hearing this woman's moaning cry for help in the complex behind us. All she keeps saying is, "Help, help, help me." My mother, Rita, lies in the bed next to the window where I am kneeling and she says nothing. She can't. I wonder from time to time what she's thinking but I don't ask because I'm afraid of her answer. Every now and again she'll say "Phyllis, go try and lay down. Please." But I can't. I think if I fall asleep that I would wake up underwater. All I can hear is the water lapping up against the building. I can't see it but it seems to be rising each second and I cannot close my eyes.

So I start praying out loud. It doesn't matter who hears me. I just want God to hear me and get us out of there. He is listening, but it isn't time for us to go. Not yet. So I pray and I beg and pray and beg. No one tries to stop me, I believe, because they know that I need to do this or else I will either lose my mind or simply die. And I think they need to hear it too.

Somehow morning comes, and it's our third day stuck in the apartment complex after the storm hit. Overnight the water had gotten higher. I can tell because I'm using the waterline on the laundry room wall. Our complex is made of mostly red brick and yellow wood. We have a pool, a playground, and a reception hall for family functions that overlooks the pool area. There is a mix of small families with kids, married couples with no kids, and elderly people. The atmosphere is comfortable and people say "Good morning" and "Hello" to each other. The grounds are always kept clean and the grass always has a rich green, almost country feeling. All of this changed on August 29, 2005.

Now we are surrounded by water. Black, foul-smelling water that smelled of shit and piss, dead bodies, just pure and sure death. I sit on the balcony of my mother's apartment, building C-71, just looking at the black water. People around me are doing the necessary things for getting food and water to keep us going. At one point Ron goes into the water to go back to our apartment to get a grill that we'd purchased a month before, so that we can cook and warm some of the food we have left. I walk to the end of the balcony to watch him. I'm afraid that something will bite him because we don't know what is in the water. We've heard that there are alligators and snakes in the water because the rivers have broken through the levees.

At first I didn't want him to go in and pleaded with him not to. But Ron kept telling me that it was okay and that he'd be okay. So I sit there on the steps wondering if this will be the last time I see my husband. Yelling at him the whole time to be careful and walk this way or walk that way. He has to walk slowly because there are boards with nails in them and we cannot afford to have him step on them without any medication. He finally makes it there and then I become filled with fear that he will fall through the floor of the apartment with all the water coming into our apartment and soaking the floor. So I keep saying that's enough time to be in the apartment. Plus the ceilings have come down and I don't know what Ron will be facing when he goes in there and I'm afraid he won't come out.

I sit and sit in the hot sun, sweat dripping down my face, most of it from fear and the heat. Ron says it didn't take him that long but to me he seemed to be in there for hours. I begin to see other people walking in the water, going from apartment to apartment finding diapers for babies and milk to feed them. People are yelling to one another from balconies to see what each person's situation is and try to get some to come to a better spot. I swear, twenty-four hours seemed like forty-eight each day.

Now we can hear the constant sound of helicopters and see them, but they won't come near us. Ron gets back safely, so we begin to heat the food with coals and eat. For a minute it seems okay but reality kicks in really quick. I walk down to the end of the balcony and attempt to speak with some guys who are held up in an apartment across from our building in the complex but they don't speak back. I learn that they do not live in the apartment but simply need somewhere to stay and have found a safe place. At least safer than where they've come from. The look in their eyes scares me because I've never seen them in the complex before. I'm glad for once for the water because it's between us and it would be hard for them to get to us—possible but hard. I walk away from them slowly, trying to think of a way to protect myself in case they try to hurt my family or me.

Upon returning to the apartment I learn that Ron and the guys have heard that the national guard is giving out food from a reception hall up the street, and they are planning to go there. A new wave of grief is what I begin to feel. I tell you it was one after another. I'm like, finish me off why don't cha? Shit, this is getting to be too much. As much as I try to come up with reasons for Ron not to go, he is determined. Then Catherine walks up to me saying that she's going to walk back to her home and get a boat my cousin has in his yard. He lives next door, but he and his family left before the storm. She will have to walk a mile from here to there. Walk in the water two blocks, then walk on the levee for a mile. She doesn't know what her block or area looks like. She has a cast on her arm because of a broken finger and has asked me to help tie a rag around her pants because she's lost a lot of weight and her pants are beginning to fall from her body. So I help her. (She later told me that's when she knew that my mental state was not good, because I didn't offer to come with her or try to stop her.) I am just mechanical in my actions. I am functioning in a daze. The world that I have lived in now looks like a bomb has been dropped on it, and nobody is coming to help. Nobody. My husband has left. My sister has left. And I don't know what's going to happen next.

Our neighbors are still listening to their radio and I walk back and forth by them to listen and get any updated information that the news is giving. They're saying that another levee has broken and more water is coming. I fear for the lives of my husband and sister but can't do anything to help them. I can't even help myself. I don't think of my mother and how she is doing: she isn't saying much and I don't ask.

The diapers from the children are piling up and the heat is making the already bad smell worse. I'm still praying not to have a heart attack because this would have killed my mother. I was thinking that if we would have left her here she would have died. Now I know we are not going to leave her. I mean she's my mom, how could I? How could we? So we wait for Ron and Catherine to come back. I continue to search for something to take to bring my heart rate down and come up empty. Ron and the others finally come back. They have water, liquor, food, and cigarettes. I see a bottle of Wild Turkey and reach for it. I find a cup and began pouring the liquor. I drink until I feel its effect. My heart begins to slow down. I drink some more. My heart slows a bit more. Then, lo and behold! My spirits pick up. What a surprise! I laugh and talk. I start organizing and cleaning up the apartment. I don't smell so bad after all. Ask me how long this feeling lasted? A few damn hours. Yep. A few damn hours. Then I think that I will want to try to liquor some more, but don't. Now, this is a first!

I find that my heart rate had returned to being rapid and high again. So again I search for pills that have sedatives in them. They seem to last longer. Six hours later my sister Catherine returns. She had tried to use the boat with the help of a neighbor, but it didn't work out. She said her home didn't get that much water but wind damage was bad. So we are back to square one. Back to anticipating another night in hell. We talk and try to keep each other's spirits going but I just really don't care anymore. I have been a fighter all of my life and have overcome many other storms, but this one has taken me out and is about to bury me. All of a sudden we hear helicopters. I run and get a broomstick and a white towel and write SOS on one side and Help on the other side. I begin running to the end of the balcony of my mom's apartment building and waving it like a crazy woman. The helicopter has seen us. We are going to be saved! Well, they come right down into the complex in front of our faces. Looking at us, a man turns to his buddy and gives the signal to pull up. They fucking leave us. That's it. I can't take any more, this is crazy. What is going on? Night falls. We go back to our positions on the floor, with the windows in the front closed. The sweat and stink are pouring from our bodies. We are hungry, funky, and thirsty. We have to do something to get out of here and fast. I go back to my craziness of shining the flashlight out the window each time I hear a helicopter. I actually believe that the pilots will see it. At some point we have to pile tables and blocks to keep Nicholas from falling out the bedroom window. The woman in the complex behind us is still yelling for help only this time her voice is hoarse and weaker, like she is losing hope. I want to help, but I can't. Catherine hears a man across the street doing the same thing: yelling for someone to help him. We pace back and forth in the apartment and pray the entire night. Some sleep for a while, some pray. I have never begged for daylight so much.

Monday, August 29

Levees in New Orleans are breached, flooding parts of the city.

**5** Katrina had won. She had succeeded in breaking my soul, and now she was going after my body too. I saw myself walking down those stairs into the water. Instead of letting her waters swallow me, I was going to swallow it and just go into the flow of death and into a new life. But God had a better plan for me. I'm writing this so I know that ultimately He (God) won.

How could our government, president, governor, mayor, and the political leaders of our country do this to us? I start thinking about the few days before, when my cell phone had some charge left and I tried to call for help. The operator said that she couldn't transfer the call to 911. Why? I had heard on the news before we lost electricity that 911 services would not be available to the people who had chosen to stay behind and ride out the storm. After trying about fifty times to dial 911 and the call wouldn't go through I hung up and dialed zero for the operator and asked her to transfer my call to 911 and she said the service was down and she couldn't put my call through. Then rumors were flowing through the apartment complex that 911 services were cut off by the city, but nobody could confirm exactly who had done it, but you could still hear people calling in to 911. In the aftermath it became easier to understand that 911 was overwhelmed with calls and I just couldn't get through to them. There were people in worse situations than mine, like the woman who called in to 911 and got through to the operator and she was in her attic with her infant child and the water was rising up to the attic and all the 911 operator could tell her was that help was on the way. And then the woman in the attic just gave up and laid her baby in the water and then herself and they both drowned while the operator was on the phone. How could they cut off 911? How could they not even let the operators transfer a call for help to 911? I was saying to the operator that I am a person, a living breathing person with a heart beating inside of a body, and you can't help me?

Jesus, please bring the morning. Please! I can't take this anymore!!!! Or, Kill Me Now. Just don't let this torture go on anymore. I can't take this. I pray through the night and I'm on my knees at the window in my mom's bedroom listening for the helicopters. I can hear Catherine's truck bumping against the Dumpster because it is floating. We can't even use that to get out. Finally after I died over and over again all night, morning begins to show her merciful face. And I hate that bitch. I love her and I hate her, but the love is more important right now because as long as I see her morning glory, I'm still alive and have been given another chance. Now it's now time to get the fuck out of here. By any means necessary, today is the day.

We all get together and start coming up with a plan. After tossing around this and that we decide to use refrigerators from a few of the first-floor apartments as floating devices to get us to dry ground. Now, it's only one block, but it's one long-ass block to dry ground. Getting from here to there will take monumental effort. We don't know what's in the water. We're taking our lives into our own hands.

My mother, Rita, has to be spoken to very calmly as we explain what we are about to do. She will have to put on a life preserver. The water is not too high, we explain. We then tell her that we have to walk one block, but it's not a straight shot. We have to walk down the steps into the water. We then have to walk out the back of the complex and across a large lot and then we'll be on dry land.

Let me tell you, it was easy while we were still standing on the balcony, above the water. But actually going down those steps was another matter. I keep going back into my mom's apartment for things I so-called forgot. What I'm really doing is trying to avoid getting into the water. I'm afraid that something like an alligator or a snake or a rat will bite me. But I don't say anything, I just go along keeping it all in my mind. It's like it's okay to think something as long as nobody knows what you are thinking. I don't know if you have ever felt anything like this: you're in a bad situation and you know that you will need to leave it at some point in time but you're also afraid of where you'll go after leaving this bad situation. Sound crazy to you? Well, that's what the hell was in my mind.

So, we all get together and start walking down the stairs into the black water. My heart is racing, so fast I think I've already gotten to Haynes Boulevard and we haven't even gotten down the stairs yet. Now I'm thinking, okay, this is the same water that people were pissing in, spitting in, and God knows what else. You would think that they would have gone to another part of the water to do this but they did it right where we lived and we have to walk in that shit. Anyway. Water up to the ankles, then the waist, then up to our chests. Shit man, this is crazy; I want to go back up the steps. But I can't. I can't go back and I don't want to go forward. I don't want to end up floating dead in this water. Not like this Lord, please not like this. I'm in. We're all in and everybody is walking like fucking zombies, all slow and shit. I'm in a hurry to get out, looking around like a crazy woman. I walk and rush but still careful that nothing comes up on me and bites me. God that was the longest walk that I have ever done in my life! I'm holding on to Ron. I'm making sure to keep an eye on my momma and making sure that Catherine and Nicholas are moving at the same pace that we are. I look around at the buildings and see Catherine's truck floating, bumping up against the complex Dumpster, Nick's clothes in the back of the truck. I look to see if I can see the lady who was calling for help in the night, wondering if she had drowned. I don't hear her while we are walking. Maybe she's fallen asleep. Maybe she's dead. We're holding on to the refrigerators to make sure the elderly and children are safe and don't tip over. My God, why is it taking so long to walk just one freaking block?

We get to the end of the back of the complex and have to step up before we get to this large, grassy lot and then to dry land on Haynes Boulevard. There are these boards that we have to step on, and spiders and big-ass fire ants are everywhere. They're all over my pants leg. I lose it. I start screaming and yelling. Ron tries to calm me down, but I am not having it. But eventually, I do calm down. We get everybody up the small step and we're on our way. I'm thinking, we got out. It's finally over. Oh, but was I in for a rude awakening. It was only just beginning. Actually, we had a lot of "beginnings." It was like we got through this and it's over, only to be faced with another "beginning." I was getting so tired of this shit, man.

Everybody starts saying different ideas of what we should do and where and how we should go about getting out of the complex because it's clear that help is not coming. Some ideas are for half of us to go out and see if there's dry land away from the complex. Some say a few of the men should go and try to find more food, water, and supplies like bathroom tissue. Some offer that we should all go at once at a certain time and use refrigerators as floating devices for the elderly and children. All of a sudden everybody's a savior. It goes from We got a safe place to go, to Oh, we can't go there, too much water in the house. I swear, my mind is like, if I had a gun I probably would just shoot all of the know-it-alls and go out into Lake Pontchartrain. Some are close friends and some are not, but we all live in the same apartment complex. Plain and simple. It's like everybody has a better plan than the next person.

All I want is to get the hell out of here and live. That's all. So we all walk across this big empty lot outside of the complex and all seems to be going in order. My mom and I get to the next block and she has to sit down right away. Catherine and Nicholas arrive and she's trying to keep him occupied. So I take him and start walking with him outside of the complex. Ron spots a heavy equipment machine and says he has the keys to start it up. Crane operators have master keys to most machines that they use.

There are still a lot of people left behind in the complex and he wants to go and bring them to dry land. Everybody's saying for him to get the machine and go back. I'm thinking about my husband and the police and his safety. I keep telling him not to go because if the police come and arrest him nobody who was telling him to go and do it would get him out of jail. Well, Ron convinces me that he needs to go and help those who were still in the complex. I have no choice but to shut up. I have no energy left to argue. So he leaves and then back and forth he goes bringing elderly people and little children to where we are.

There is this home, a very large, beige-and-gray brick home. It has black security bars on all of the windows and doors. There is a silver-colored metal shed in the backyard and on the front lawn there is a statue of Mary, the mother of Jesus, where we sit to catch our breath and rest a minute until everybody arrives. While my mom is sitting I make a weak effort to relieve Catherine in helping with Nicholas. Nick and I walk back and forth to keep him busy. One of the trials of autism is restlessness and with Nick he likes to keep moving or doing something. The worst part for me is seeing his lips dry—cracked from lack of drinking water. After growing tired myself, I turn Nick back over to Catherine. I walk over to where my mom is sitting, and just begin looking around at the devastation. I mean it's like, I know we just walked away from death but we're still walking into death.

I'm becoming anxious again, because Ron is taking so long to come back. I start walking back toward the lot that leads to the apartment complex but cannot walk too close to where we've just come from. It's too much for me. I don't want to go back there because it's filled with too much pain. So I stand right at the edge of these people's property and the lot. I start yelling Ron's name. I'm against him going back because I don't want him to get into any trouble. Everybody's yelling for him to go and "do this" or "do that." I don't like that nobody else is doing anything and they're pushing for Ron to do it. After all, he's my husband and damn it if I say let's go I think he should go. But that's not how Ron's heart is and it's the reason why I first fell in love with him and still do. He puts everybody else before him and goes without until the other person is complete.

After the last run he makes going back to the apartment complex, I begin to feel some relief. Well, that doesn't last long. You see, I'm thinking that Ron's finished saving people, and we will hold hands and walk on to being saved. Oh, but no. Some people cannot walk that well, my momma being one of them. Now, don't get me wrong. I care about people, but I'm like, just let us get the fuck out of here. I gotta be honest with you. I mean we got them to dry land, so what more are we supposed to do? One of the many things that I learned during this disaster is that whatever your nature is, you cannot fight it. No matter how badly I wanted us to get out of there, we could not leave people behind. It wouldn't have been right, simple and plain. So Ron begins loading people up on the machine and bringing them to the Nazareth Inn, an elderly home located on Haynes Boulevard. We are told that we will be safe there and can bed down for the night and get some food and water.

While Ron is earning his wings to heaven, I on the other hand am saying, I am not walking up Haynes where all of these power lines are lying in the street. Ron's telling me that there is no electricity in them because the city has no power. Whatever! I am not risking getting electrocuted! Ron is still trying to convince me that it is safe to walk on the ground. Hell no! So I begin my journey up the levee on Haynes with my little suitcase, looking like a runaway child, only I'm in my forties. Ain't that some shit? Well, call it what you want, I didn't drown and I'm damn sure not going to be electrocuted. So I'm walking up the levee. As I start up the steps a woman and her elderly mother are doing the same thing. Although I don't know if it's for the same reason that I'm doing it. All I know is that I am once again about to come back to my true nature. I mean this woman is about eighty years old: y'all, how do you turn away from that? You don't. You can't. I can hear the woman telling her mother to keep on going and they will be picked up at UNO (University of New Orleans at the Lakefront). Now, we are at Read Boulevard and Haynes Boulevard. UNO is about four miles from where we are. I'm thinking how in the hell is the old lady going to make it that far? Then she's thirsty.

I stop and tell the daughter to let me help her carry the bags to the top of the levee and that I have a bottle of water that her mother can have. Once we get to the top of the levee she allows her mother to rest and once I give her the water, I begin my walk to being saved.

My state of mind while walking is in many, many places, people. I'm thinking about a lot of things that I did as a child. Like playing ball, jacks, and sitting on the porch waiting for the ice cream truck to come by in our neighborhood. The smells of the grass in Easton Park back a town by Bayou St. John, where we grew up. I think about my "real" daddy and how I will never get to meet him, and my stepdad whom I love, also my grandma and grandpa, my aunt Madeline, and just crazy stuff. I also think about if I make it out of this shit how I will kick the asses of our city leaders and world leaders for leaving us to die. I mean I honestly think of how I will meet these people and just straight up knock them the fuck out! Then I think about what will happen to me if I do these things. But it does help me from going crazy up there on the levee.

I remember imagining me and Governor Blanco fighting, and when I went to pull her hair it came off in my hands. I told her that I knew all the time that she wore a wig. Then I scratched her face or tried to and my fingernails kept getting filled up with makeup and I couldn't get to her real skin. Which now that I think about it kind of gives you confirmation that politicians don't really show you what's behind the face. Do they ever tell the truth? I could never marry a politician for that same reason. I would never know who it was that I was sleeping with, you know? So I'm walking on the levee and the mud is kicking up on the back of my shirt and my tennis shoes are deep in mud and at the same time I'm thinking that I want to thank Payless Shoe Source because, contrary to what people say, those cheap-ass tennis shoes are sure holding up for me.

I look down and there are about fifty to seventy-five people in my immediate area, and behind them there are more people, hundreds of black faces migrating to higher ground and obviously nobody has come to help them either because they are carrying blankets and bottles of water and pillows. Some have placed their belongings in green garbage bags and have them thrown across their shoulders while they walk in the street below. Those who are walking on the levee where I am are dragging their bags through the grass and mud, too tired to even care that the bags are getting holes in them and their clothes are becoming muddy and wet. Then I see Ron going back to the complex on the machine he tells me later is a front-end loader and that's exactly what he's doing: loading people on the front end of this machine and bringing them to safety. I stop and look at him and my heart begins to feel something good because he's doing something good. I walk some more and then I stop again because I'm worried that something will happen to him, but I see him smile and wave to some people and I know that he's okay. I keep on walking and I see the Nazareth Inn. Great! We're saved!

I walk down the steps of the levee, and even though I feel relief I also feel stupid that I thought that I would be electrocuted. Once I get down to the ground in front of the Nazareth Inn and meet up with my family, I begin to ask where

Ron is. I walk up Haynes and see Ron walking. I ask why he's walking and he tells me that the machine's tire went flat and he returned it to where he got it. So we walk into the Nazareth Inn to see what's going on, and see that these people are in worse-off trouble then we are. The elderly and sick are sitting outside in wheelchairs and on benches. Neighbors of my mom had told us about this place and said that it would be a good spot to get food and somewhere decent to sleep, etc. Not! We walk inside and this is where a little of my "breakdown" starts to show, only I don't realize this until after everything's over. There's no electricity, or hot water, and there's water damage in the entire building. But somehow these women are in the kitchen cooking, and I still to this day don't remember how they were doing what they were doing. My mom's neighbor starts giving out orders as to who goes where and so on. Then she says the words that pulled out my "Indian blood." She says: "I'm the Big Chief in here." Hold up. I look at her and I say, "Who in the hell made you Chief? Baby, I'm my own chief and it don't go that way."

Now, don't get me wrong, this woman had a Bible in her hand and sometimes she would just place it down on something and let it lay open to a particular scripture or psalm, from the time I first met her until the end, and she helped me a whole lot by reading and quoting scripture to me. She was a very important part of my sanity, but in just that one moment I could not have someone attempting to take control over what was left of my life. It's not in my nature.

As soon as I say the words to her, she does not challenge me, she just seems to understand what is there in my state of mind. That's all. We continue from there just like nothing happened, because, in essence, nothing did.

We are all just surviving and she's helping me more than she knows. Aunt Jackie, you are my "She-ro." We have some food with us, and bring it into the kitchen, which is being run on a generator. And this is basically our trade for lodging. Then we walk into an area that seems to be the cafeteria for the residents. The carpet is soaking wet and the smell is horrible. It's the smell of wet carpet, old and musty. I'm like, okay, where's the rooms? Where are we going to sleep or take a shower? Cafeteria workers start passing out plates of food. Being honest, it looks like dog food. And this is food that they already had in the kitchen. I vow to treat others nicer—even nicer than I already did—because I do not want to end up in a place like that. I mean, it doesn't look like there's something bad going on there, it just looks like, pre-Katrina, it was not a happy place to be, and, post-Katrina, it's even more depressing. I wonder, how did these people end up being left here? It just pushes my mind into overtime. Then we finally get the answer to where we will sleep and that would be on top of tables and in chairs in the cafeteria. Baaaaaby, ain't no way. We have my mom with bad legs, Nicholas with autism, Catherine with Crohn's disease, and me on the verge of a nervous breakdown. Although right then, I actually think I'm doing okay. I don't know what the symptoms of a nervous breakdown are, so my thought process and the fact that I'm still in a mind of surviving gives me no reason for alarm. Catherine is walking back and forth outside. The rest of us are kind of walking around talking to people. Finally I eat some of the food and, just as it looks, it's horrible. Nicholas loves gravy and rice and even he only eats one spoonful of that shit. Catherine gives him a Capri drink and calls it a moment. Rita flies off the handle at this lady who's there because she keeps whining about our situation and Rita just goes off on her, telling her if she doesn't want to go with us on the truck to just stay her ass there, but shut the hell up! Catherine comes back yelling that she's found this guy with a flatbed truck rescuing people and bringing them to a helicopter pickup point at UNO Lakefront Campus. I get scared because I'm getting tired of people saying we're going to a "good spot" and it not happening. Baby, Catherine gets on that truck with Nicholas and my momma and she says, "either y'all coming or y'all staying, but we're going." So, after asking a million questions we get on the truck. Catherine says when she first went up to the driver to ask where he was going, he looked at her and asked, "You a Montana, huh?"

And that's when Catherine came to get us. Not a lot of people get on and I don't know if it's from fear or just plain being tired. While we're on the truck we start talking and it feels better because we're about to be rescued. We get to UNO and there's thousands of people there: every race, every class, and every age. There are cats, dogs, and birds in cages and these people were not leaving their pets. One lady who's with us, Karen, has a parrot. Man, is she upset when they tell her that she cannot take her bird. I mean she begs and pleads and cries, but they will not let her take her pet. She ends up having to leave the bird in the cage there on the grass. This is the first day that we are on the grounds of the campus. Then the national guard starts making us form lines to get on the helicopters. We make sure everybody has signed up with the Red Cross so our family and friends will know we are alive.

Once we get into the lines they first told us that they were not going to separate families. It's a lie. We're all standing together, all five of us: me, Ron, Catherine, Rita, and Nicholas. Guy walks up to us and we tell him that we are all family and that we have to stay together. The same guy walks away, telling us that we'll be on the next helicopters. Helicopters come in, we get happy, and then he puts his arm in between us and tells us that he can take my momma, my sister, and my nephew because they are taking the elderly, sick, and children first. I tell my sister to go ahead and that we are going to be okay because the guy told us we'd be next to go. Our "next to go" never came. It never came. This fool-ass man got us standing in line telling us to wait and we'll be next and like damn fools we stood there with funky, stinky-smelling water on our bodies.

I was hungry and tired, but always hopeful. Does this make any sense? Hope is really what kept us alive. The Reverend Jesse Jackson really helped me. I remembered what he said, but reversed it. *Hope* kept *me* alive. I look around, and the sun is setting over the trees and I am imagining us sitting out on the lake on a Sunday afternoon. Cool winds blowing and the music in the air, just chillin'. But this is not Sunday on the Lakefront. This is survival and, I'm not going to lie, I'm getting tired, hopeful but tired. When it finally dawns on us that we are going to have to sleep on the grass, my breathing gets easy. It's better to know and not be guessing. So I find a few garbage bags for Ron to sleep on because that grocery basket that he's sitting and falling asleep on is not going to do it. Yes, he's actually sitting up on a grocery basket sleeping while I sit on the ground next to him to keep him from falling over. I take a walk around the grounds and it's horrific!

There is an open building on the grounds, and I think it would work as a place to crash because they have reclining chairs, but the smell is too much to bear. It smells like people were using the bathroom on the floors so I quickly get out of there. When I go back to where Ron and my mom's neighbors are, Ron is still sitting up on the grocery basket, the metal kind that's small enough for a young child to fit inside of, but if you lay it on its side you can sleep on it, depending on your size. Ron just sits upright on it and sleeps. I have to convince him to get down and sleep on the trash bags. Finally he does, and immediately falls asleep. I stay up talking to our neighbors, and once everybody starts to fall asleep, a strange thing happens to me.

I haven't mentioned this to anyone until now. As I look into the dark over the grounds and the bodies sleeping on the grass, I see what appears to be water. It's black water, and the waves are moving really slowly back and forth. Then I hear a voice telling me to come in. I blink my eyes and shake my head because I know that my imagination is getting the best of me. I look again and the black water is calling to me again to come in. My heart begins to race and when I look around again, there I am: the only one out there on the grounds. I get to my knees and feel like I want to walk into those black waters and fall asleep. Then, something inside of me stops. I don't know why but my sense of being comes back. I lean against Ron's back and fall asleep counting the stars in the sky, thinking how much my life has changed and wondering what will happen next. Sleep comes and goes because I am on constant guard about someone stealing what little we have left. Morning takes so long to arrive I often wonder if it ever will.

Tuesday, August 30

Efforts to close a two-block-wide breach in a levee at the 17th Street Canal fail. 80 percent of the city is flooded.

**6** This is day five, no bath nor opportunity to brush my teeth. Just pure wilderness. We are like animals in the wild and nobody cares but us if we survive. The sounds of helicopters are in the distance and this really begins to wake everyone up and get their things in order. There's trash and filth everywhere. It reminds me of the aftermath of a concert when trash, cans, and rotten food are left all over the place. So we get up, and the cattle calls are being made for us to get into lines to be "rescued."

Ron looks terrible. He, like the rest of us, is not used to sleeping on the ground, and why should he be? We're supposed to be sleeping in our beds like human beings. Once people are in the lines, the helicopters begin landing and calls are made for people to board. After several lines have left and we have not been chosen to board, I ask why. The fire department and national guard are in control of the helicopters landing and the people boarding. But there is a young black guy making the actual calls and contacting the people in the lines. I think he is part of their personnel. He's doing a pretty good job of keeping things in order and adding a little bit of humor to the situation. I later found out, when we got to San Antonio, that he was in the same situation as we were and was just a regular evacuee, because when I asked him, did he work for the city, and he said, no. My conclusion was that the firefighters and national guardsmen "appointed" him to communicate with the crowds of people.

Anyway, he's walking up and down yelling to us to make sure our lines are straight and orderly, or we won't be picked to board the helicopters. People start getting desperate and irritable, to say the least, because we can't understand how the lines are being picked. I start losing it, cussing and yelling and questioning favoritism at picking the lines. In the line next to ours a young couple has an infant child and the baby is dehydrated and turning red. What is scary about this is that the baby is dark brown and her cheeks are turning bright red. The mother starts yelling and crying that her baby is dying. The father is saying the next time the guy comes by he is going to fuck him up if they don't get on the next helicopter. He doesn't have any cigarettes, and comments that he needs a smoke. I ask Ron to walk up to him and try to calm him down. At the same time, I will get to the mother and try to calm her down. The guy who is in charge of talking to us, I'll call him Lying Larry. Larry comes by and begins to tell different people in the lines what they can and cannot bring. He tells the couple with the dying baby that they can't bring all of the bags of clothes they have with them on the helicopter. Oh, My God, she goes off.

This commotion brings the national guard a little closer to our lines. So I walk over to her and suggest first for her to let me hold the baby and she does. While I do that I tell her, fuck him and put the clothes on your body. That way when you get on the helicopter you'll have all of your clothes with you and they won't have anything to say. Same thing with the baby's diapers. Put the diapers inside of your pants, you and your old man line your underwear with the diapers. Just stuff them inside your clothes. This seems to calm them down some. Ron gives him a few cigarettes and tells him that what he is thinking about doing is only going to cause him more trouble. It is better to just try and relax. This shit is working. And it takes my mind off what we are going through.

I tell you, everybody should try helping someone else worse off than you and see how it makes your problem a little bit less important and relieves your stress. Two down, thousands to go. But we don't have the strength to go around trying to solve everyone's problems. Ron and I have agreed that if we get picked before the young couple, we'll let them go ahead of us. I hear that a couple of my relatives have been seen, but can't find them when I go to look. It takes forever for us to get out of there, and line after line is being picked ahead of us.

I finally see a cousin of mine who is with a group of girls who have babies, but I lose contact with my cousin Kizzy and the group of girls that she is with. Helicopter after helicopter comes and goes. Then we start seeing them coming into the landing area, but they aren't landing. Lying Larry comes out and says that's because people are rushing at the helicopters without their lines being called, the pilots feel threatened and won't land. We are then warned that if anyone rushes a helicopter without being called first to board, they will be shot. This is when I notice armed soldiers standing on the landing platform. They then walk away to the side of the landing platform and the helicopters begin to land and people are boarding again. But not us. I start walking up and down making sure that people are in line. This is what we have to go through, like we are in kindergarten or something. I am beginning to revert to my childhood as a safety zone. I do this by thinking of fun times like playing ball at the neighborhood park or sitting on the bayou watching the water flowing by or sitting on the porch with my sisters and friends eating crawfish or ice cream. Finally, and thank the God above, the line next to us with the young couple is called. A few hours later we are told that because it is getting dark there will be no more helicopters for the day. We will have to sleep another night on the grass, which is now wet and super funky. We go back to our "home on the range" and make our beds. This night is worse because we're hearing that some people are breaking into buildings out on the campus grounds. (I never saw anyone or knew of anyone who was doing this, but people were talking.) This brings fear, because if they are doing this then things are getting desperate again. We sit and talk until all is quiet. During the night I can hear glass breaking and see people running in the night, but I pay no attention. People are being put in a situation of pure animal survival. What's in those buildings I don't know, but when you feel you have nothing to lose you do whatever it takes to get some human feeling, and for some people stealing gives them at least some type of human feeling, I guess.

Word of mouth comes back to us that ice and food are back by the building where the chairs are. I volunteer to go and see, and all they have is, believe it or not . . . watermelon. Hot watermelon. I refuse to take it. I mean, if there was ever confirmation that we were being thought of as niggers, this is it. Watermelon! All we need now are fields of cotton. We already have Lying Larry as the overseer. We have the black bodies and my cousin named Kizzy. The only thing missing is Kunta Kinte saying don't call him Toby.

Sleep apparently comes because we wake up the next morning surrounded by the filth of yesterday. Again we form the lines and again we watch sadly as all others are being loaded onto the helicopters. Again we are threatened with guns and being shot if we rush the helicopters. Again the helicopters feel so threatened that they won't land.

Then comes the blow to the heart. Lying Larry comes out and calls for quiet on the plantation. Larry advises us that there will be no more rescue attempts by helicopter or boat. He says that we have to find a way to get to the Lakefront Airport on our own, and it's four and a half miles away! He tells us late in the evening that the helicopters will be doing rescues in the morning for the last time. So, if we don't get there by morning we'll be stuck right here on the campus grounds with no hope of being rescued and no one having any knowledge of us even being there.

In the meantime someone has a radio and Mayor C. Ray

Nagin is heard crying and saying that we need help down here. He's cussing and going on and on. This woman runs up to me and tells me what is going on and that the mayor really cares about us and so on and I just look at her in pure amazement and say, "Are you fucking crazy! Do you realize how many days we've been out in the streets, abandoned? And moreover, how do you know that he's actually crying? He's on the radio, for God's sake!" I try to understand the logic behind the mayor's speech and the woman's faith in him but it never happens.

I have since forgiven all those who left us. If I don't my life will forever be stuck inside of the levees that broke. It did not have to be this way.

We get the word from the "appointed" guy that there are to be no more rescue attempts for us. The people who are left there along with our group start picking up their belongings, food, and supplies that are left over since we've been there so that we can start our journey to the last rescue pickup spot that we have to walk to. People are getting their things in order, some things necessary to take, some just bullshit. Some people tell Ron to go and get this machine and we could ride on it to the Lakefront Airport. I point blank say hell no. Night is beginning to fall. I look at Ron and tell him, "Let's giddy the fuck up"—those are my exact words and we start walking. We aren't really leaving the others, just getting a head start. I am afraid, especially because we are starting to hear that another levee has breached and water will soon be filling up the area we are in and we will drown if we stay. So I tell Ron that he is not taking any machine and we start to walk.

I am walking fast, I mean really fast. I'm okay as long as I know Ron is right behind me. His feet are blistered from the toes to the heel. I don't care. I just want to get to the rescue spot before morning. But no matter how fast I walk I can't walk faster than the sun is setting and before long it's dark and we've just reached the Franklin Avenue part of the lakefront. While we are walking I look behind me and see this long line of people. I am walking so fast that I have to look back and see where Ron is. He isn't far behind but his feet are so blistered that my heart is breaking with each step that I take. City trucks and levee police are passing us by and I start running up to them begging for a ride to the Lakefront Airport but they say they can't stop. I figure if I keep asking, one of them will give in and give us a ride. Ron yells at me from behind to stop asking. I ask one more, then I stop. My heart rate is rising again so I slow my walking pace down.

By the time we get midway across the lakefront it's pitch black. I lose my sense of direction but Ron remembers how to get there. We have to walk over the Seabrook Bridge to get to the other side because under the bridge there's about ten to twelve feet of water. I don't know how I hold it together but I do. Once we get down to the bottom of the bridge we have to climb over the railing to get to the ground. Each person who does this slips down, as there is thick mud on the ground. Ron climbs over before me, warning me to be careful of the mud.

Just as I've climbed over the railing, a woman in a red dress comes from out of nowhere yelling and screaming for us not to go on any further because she has heard the government is setting us up to go this way and is planning to open the floodgates to drown us. Everybody, I mean everybody stops dead in their tracks. She repeats what she's just said and one by one people just start going on to the airport. I gotta say she scared the living hell out of me. I start yelling at Ron that I can't see, and how are we going to get through this side of the bridge when we can't see a damn thing. Of course he reassures me that he knows where he is going, and there is also a line of people in front of us who are ending up on the other side. The only lights we have are small flashlights and a lantern.

That's when I'm reminded of the Underground Railroad. I'm serious. It's like we are runaway slaves on the damn Underground Railroad. Ms. Harriet Tubman must be looking over us, because we start getting closer and closer. But it seems to take so long. Like, the closer we get the further away the airport tower is from us. We connect back with my mother's neighbors and everyone is okay. I keep wondering if I will die by drowning or starvation. Then my mind becomes tired and I just walk and go wherever I am told to go. I don't care anymore. And the weird thing about all of these thoughts is that one minute I am giving up, and the next minute, I am determined to survive.

Once we get to the rescue site there are hundreds, maybe thousands of people sleeping on the ground.

Wednesday, August 31

Governor Blanco asks the president for forty thousand federal troops.

7 There are trucks giving out MREs, some type of military food that has this self-heating device. At that point I think I'd eat uncooked red beans and rice. It's that bad. The lines are too long so we continue to walk until we find a spot to sleep for the night. My hope begins to rise again because it seems real and we are going to get the care that we need. Wrong! The only spot that we are able to find is on concrete, because all of the grass spots have been taken. I volunteer—or am chosen— to go and get food for everybody. I walk all the way back to the point where we came in and get in line. I tell the man how many people are with us, and add a few extra numbers so we can get more food, and plus we don't know if we are really going to get out or how long it will take. But he only gives me what he thinks I need, which is fine with me. Shit, things are getting better by the minute and for all I care he

can go fuck himself. Of course, this is my thinking after I get the food. Ain't this some bullshit? I got to bargain for food? Oh, my God! This is serious. I keep saying to myself, "Wake up, Phyllis, wake up." I know I'm awake and I know we're in trouble: now, days before, and with more to come. I think it will get worse before it gets better and guess what? It does.

Okay, so I get back with the "food," and morale has picked up so much that for a minute I think we're out camping and this is supposed to be fun. Ron's lying on the ground trying to get comfortable. Planes and helicopters are landing, but they're not there to take anyone. At least not just yet. It's like pouring buckets of crawfish in front of someone born and raised in New Orleans and telling them they can have the claws, but leave the tail and the head. Once everyone eats his or her rations I decide to take a walk around to see what the situation looks like. It reminds me of a *Twilight Zone* movie where you can see what's happening around you and everything seems real, even to the touch, but on the outside there's a giant and you're the dolls in a house. Then what used to be something you could confront head on you now run from and fear. The good thing is when you remember God in the same way, it can turn a bad thing into a good thing. How many of us living and breathing can say they have seen God? But don't we still believe in Him? I know I do.

Thursday, September 1

State officials prevent the Red Cross from entering
New Orleans with food and water, so as not to get
in the way of military operations. The Department of
Defense begins assembling active-duty troops.

Everybody survived Hurricane Katrina. Everybody. The levees breaking is what killed all those people. It's a damn shame that we can't hold the corps of engineers responsible for the lost lives, the unnecessary loss of lives due to its negligence. There is a God above and like His Word says, "Vengeance is mine, says the Lord." Don't worry, Judgment Day is a reality and His Will Be Done.

I'm walking around taking in all of this misery, suffering, and pain into my spirit, hoping that it will lessen some of the pain that my people, that all of New Orleans have to deal with. I get to the end of the helicopter runway, and I'm looking out over the lake, and it's just too soon for me to go. It's just too soon. I've got work to do. I get back to our "lodgings" and Ron is half asleep, half awake, wondering where I've gone. I can't say I sleep, but Ron does the best that he can. It isn't long before law enforcement comes and tells us that we have to move back because we are sleeping on the actual runway and it's dangerous. We move back further on the concrete. In the morning we have to form lines again, and I swear it takes so long that I'm about to run out on the runway and fall on my knees begging to be let on the damn helicopter. We finally get picked. Don't know how or why. Don't care. I know y'all won't believe this but I could swear that the guy on the helicopter is Tom Cruise when he played in *Top Gun*. Call me crazy, call me what you want. You have your fantasy of rescue, and I'll have mine. The look in his eyes is so sincere, it's like he's a part of my real family. (Ron says that they were national guardsmen. Now them I love. Really, I don't have any bad memories of them in particular. It's just that I wish people would bend rules sometimes; it could save lives, and someone's sanity. But all in all, I began to feel the healing.)

Does it last long? Helllllll no! So, I'm thinking, "We're outta here, suckas!" When we're up in the air we can see the city, and man, I didn't know there was so much water in the city, and I think about how much damage Hurricane Katrina has done. Little do I know. Oh, but little do I know.

I'm thinking that we're on our way out of the city, especially since I see all of that water. In about ten or fifteen minutes the pilot of the helicopter is signaling the other guy that we are due for landing. I'm like, "Damn, that was quick!" Because we have been hearing that people are going to Texas and other places and I think, that was a helluva ride. We're in Texas already? Ask me where we get dropped off? Just ask me. They drop us off at the Armstrong Airport!

In New Orleans! We are still in the city! Okay. We haul our tired, stinky asses off the helicopter. They tell us where to go. And again, there's a line. But this time it's a little bit different. We walk into the airport and there's people lying all around on the filthy floors. It does not even look like an airport.

People have makeshift beds in corners. We have been warned early on not to go into the restrooms, because there's piss and shit all over the floors and in the sinks. People have had nowhere to empty their bowels, so when they ran out of toilets they were shitting in the restroom sinks, and when that ran out they started shitting on the floors until there is so much shit nobody can go in there. That's why I was so pissed off when the guy who ran the airport gave public testimony in Spike Lee's *When the Levees Broke* that "everything ran smoothly and there were no problems at the airport." I wanted to put my whole leg up his ass, let alone my foot. Lying mutherfucker.

We get into the airport and guess who I see. The young couple who were yelling and screaming that their child was dying. I walk up to the woman and ask how her baby is doing. She says, oh, he's fine. I try to remind her of where I know her from and she just says that the baby is fine. Well, you gotta know me to understand me. I press on until she remembers being in the line next to us and she remembers me. I tell her of everything that happened, and you know what? She says, "Oh, my baby was fine the whole time, I just wanted to get the fuck out of there." All righty, now. No hate. Do what you gotta do, girlfriend, I say to myself. Then, I move on.

We find a spot to camp out on the ground against the escalators and out of the way of people walking up and down in front of us. Some are lying on the floor against the wall on the other side of the floor across from us. The floors are filthy and muddy and stink like urine and feces, but we sit anyway. So, the adults are saying that they and the children with us are hungry and I've seen someone passing by with a brown bag that was filled with a sandwich and chips, cookies and soda. I ask where they got it from and am told that a food stand has been set up to feed us, so we walk over to get food for our group. I don't know what it is with me but for some strange reason I will go for food. I think I volunteer this time. Man, there are so many people there, it does not make any sense. No sense at all. None. I find the food line and the line is very, very long and the people in the line are angry, hungry, and scared at the situation we are in. I stay in that line for what must be at least three hours. Then the line is split into two and I am left farther back than where I've been standing, but I have to stay: we are starving. But again, the worst part is seeing the restaurants that are normally there in real time. Places that sold oyster po'boys.

My momma told me a long time ago that in New Orleans during the Depression, they could buy a loaf of French bread for a nickel and put cold cuts on it and it would feed an entire family. Anyway, that's a po'boy. They started calling it that because it was what "po'folks" were buying. Now it's one of the most highly sought-after foods in New Orleans.

I'm looking at all of these restaurants and thinking to myself that I would sell my husband for a oyster po'boy dressed with extra pickles. (Not really, but keeping it real, baaaaby, it sure sounded good at the time.) I get in the food line and have the nerve, once I get to the front of the line, to ask if they had any Cheetos. Only because I've seen other people making requests. But I've forgotten I'm not in that class. The people who are giving out the food bags are mostly white and the people making requests for a particular type of cookie or chips are being satisfied and when the black people ask for the same they are told that they can only get what is left over, but then another white person requests their choice and gets it. I saw this with my own two weary eyes. I just take what is given to me and walk away, feeling somewhat shameful and honestly, like a nigger, an animal. I am there for quite some time, obviously, because when I get out of the line and am on my way back to the group I see Ron standing there waiting for me. The closer I get to him the better I can hear him asking, what took you so long? Then I see: tears. They are flowing down my baby's face and my heart is no more. Let me explain. Ron is the absolute love of my entire life. When he is hurt, and I don't care by whom, it's going down. You hear me? I ask him what's wrong. He asks me again why I took so long. I answer that there was a long line and I had to get food for everyone. Ron looks me in my eyes, and I don't even think that he even knows he's been crying. He says, "They left us." I yell, "Who?" The people we were with had gotten in a line that was boarding people on the planes to leave out. I yell, "They left us? I went to get food for them!" I tell Ron, you know what? That's okay. They did what they felt they had to do. Not a problem.

The good thing is that, if things had happened differently,

if we'd gotten on that plane, I wouldn't be where I'm at right now, in New Orleans, my home. So, thank you to all who made this story what it is, be it negative or positive. I don't hold anything against anybody and one day we can all have dinner at my house, on me. It's that kind of love. And, another thing: Ron and I didn't let those bologna sandmiches go to waste. Yeah, I spelled them just how we say it: sandmiches.

Anyway. After we finish eating we hear that planes are starting to board and we have to get in line. Here we go. We are on our way, baby. I'm thinking we get in line and get on the plane. Kinda like "Getting on The Bus." So we get in line. Or what is supposed to be a line. People are skipping. The lines are getting mixed in with other lines. It is total chaos. We just go where we think we are supposed to go.

After a few hours the crowd begins to get restless. We can see the elderly people lying on the floor on the other side of the room. We are in there so long I tell Ron that I am wondering how long we are going to have to stay in Charity Hospital. I actually think we are in Charity Hospital.

Friday, September 2

Governor Blanco issues an executive order
allowing out-of-state doctors not licensed in
Louisiana to provide emergency treatment.
The president proposes to the governor that
the local police and national guard be put under
federal control, to streamline the chain of command
and unify operations.

Charity Hospital in New Orleans services the poor. It's where I was born on December 24, 1963. It's a very depressing place and the airport makes me feel like we're there. This is the beginning of me having a nervous breakdown. Ron assures me that we are in the airport. We start hearing stories about the New Orleans Superdome and the Convention Center and that babies are being raped. Women are being raped and people are being murdered and people are being left to die. We hear people saying that they were actually at the Convention Center and the Superdome and saw the murders and saw the rapes, but people won't talk about it too much. There are people talking about they were the ones who beat the mutherfucker to death who raped someone. I don't know who they are, and don't know what they look like, and I don't want to know. In my personal opinion, anyone who rapes a child, a baby, needs to be put to death immediately. It just ain't right. God forgive me, but it just ain't right. Ain't enough time to wait for justice in the world for that one.

The smell. I smell them dying. Those old people who have no family members there with them. One minute you see them and know they are about to die, and the next minute they're gone. I gotta be honest, I have to lose interest if I am going to survive. It's just that the smell will never leave my mind. Never.

Now when we first get in line in front of the doors that you go through to get on the plane, to the right of us are escalators. These only have some type of military personnel in place. Then this Korean doctor is up at the top of the escalators explaining that if we are trying to reach a family member to just let them know that person's name and where to meet up and they will announce it. I want to thank one person from the bottom of my heart because he makes me and others laugh. The person sends word that they are looking for "Mike Jones" and when the doctor asks if there is a Mike Jones, the crowd answers, "Who?" and the doctor repeats "Mike Jones" and the crowd again says, "Who?" We are cracking up laughing. This comes from a rap song where this guy Mike Jones is rapping about how once he became popular, everybody was now calling his name. It just so happens that this is one of my favorite songs. It is such a small, silly thing but it helps lift our spirits—if for just a moment.

While we are standing hour after hour we see different people that we know. Ron sees some people. I see some people. I see, or think I see, a guy from my past: horrible,

horrible man. At first, I think it's my imagination. Dismissing it as such, we continue to stand. We are so thick in standing that I try several times to sit at Ron's feet, but can't because we are packed wall to wall in this airport.

Again I see this guy and this time the look on his face is as if he is trying to avoid my gaze. The third time I see him I am convinced that it is not my imagination. Katrina has in fact brought to surface all kinds of rotten things. I remember how at sixteen years of age this man beat me and was responsible for the years of tears and hurt and loneliness I experienced. I'd met him when he moved from the Desire Housing Project to our neighborhood and he was a few years older than me and he knew how to con young girls who did not have any "street smarts." All I knew was playing ball, and being damn good at it—I was the pitcher on the team all the years I played. He tricked me into thinking that I was grown and mature. Then one day we were play wrestling on the sofa in his house and I got the better of him and he slapped me in my face. I slapped him back and he slapped me harder. I became confused and told a family member, who told me to go back to his house and hit him back. Foolishly, I did, and he stood in his doorway and cussed me, calling me bitches and whores, and I did not know how to respond to this because boys we grew up with did not act that way or speak to us girls this way, and I always won fights, always. But I couldn't beat him, and Lord knows I tried.

My mistake was that I tried to resolve this problem on my own at first, then went to family members who really did not have the time or know how deep the trouble I was in, and getting deeper into. So I took the abuse. I took the beatings.

Then he started doing it more and more in public. If he told me to do something and I talked back to him or disagreed with him he'd pull his car to the side of the road and tell me to get out. As I stood on the sidewalk, he would get out of the car and smack me around and then order me back into the car and I would get in and cry and then he'd say he was sorry and that I was making him act the way he was. By this time I was filled with so much shame and confusion I just took it, because I thought nobody would care anyway.

Year after year I had no knowledge of what to do and how to get out of this life of certain destruction. I attempted suicide because I ran out of ideas of how to get away from him and thought the only way would be to kill myself, and that way he couldn't hurt me anymore. I abused drugs to dull the pain and confusion. Mostly it was sleeping pills that I would buy from the pharmacy or steal from my mom's dresser drawer. She had been prescribed sleeping pills after my stepdad died but she wasn't taking them. So I would steal them and sleep all day and stay up all night because I would have these "Freddy Krueger" nightmares. Then he would come around and bullshit me again, talking me into being with him.

I remember after the first suicide attempt, I'd taken the whole bottle of pills and woke up in the hospital after my mom found me on the living room floor and called the ambulance, and he came into the hospital room. There was a tray of food close to my bed and you know what that bastard asked me? He asked me was I going to eat because he was hungry. And he sat there and ate the food that the orderly had left for me to eat. Because he'd brainwashed me at an early age he was able to come back into my life even after that.

He continued to abuse me and I continued to take it for many years and he finally gave me some drugs one night and I fell asleep and woke up in Houston with two other girls. His mission was to make us prostitutes working for him. He conned me into thinking that I was his "number one girl" and that it was just the two other girls who would "work" for him. But he ended up trying to put me out on the streets after they snuck off and left him. It didn't work out too well and he ended up referencing this book by a guy named Iceberg Slim. In this book it taught how to beat a prostitute if she got out of line, by wrapping a towel around a wire hanger and making her strip naked and beating her so that she would not have any scars. But his comprehension was on the level of retardation and he forced me to strip naked and lie across the bed and he whipped my back with a wire hanger and told me if I got up he would kill me. So I laid there naked while he whipped me like a slave with my skin opening up. He then beat me on the top of my feet with a wooden paper towel holder and after all of this told me to come stand in front of him, and he hugged me and then asked me if I liked what he'd just done to me. I said no, and he punched me in my face. Then he asked me again if I liked what he'd just done to me and I had to say, yes. And I did say yes. His mentor was Iceberg Slim and this was done to keep my mind confused and in fear. The zero self-esteem.

All of those things come back to haunt me. More hours standing on our feet bring my attention back to the present. And I start to have panic and anxiety attacks. My breathing becomes short and labored. I tell Ron frantically how I am feeling, and I tell him that I am going to ask one of the guards if I can sit in the area where they are standing with this huge fan blowing. I don't wait for Ron's answer, and begin to fight my way through the crowd. Once I arrive at the section of fresh air I explain to the guard how I am feeling, and he says that it is okay for me to stand there a little while. I'm thinking, "All right, things are looking up again." Wrong. I have to go back to where we were standing. It takes me like fifteen or twenty minutes to fight my way through the crowd—just a few feet. That's how packed like cattle we are in there. People start getting restless again. Babies are overheated and fainting, elderly people are in the same situation and worse: they are dying. There is word that a makeshift morgue has been set up in several places to pile up the dead bodies. People start yelling and screaming for those in charge to get us out of there. Me, I keep trying to breathe, and am back and forth in the cool section. At one point I start yelling to the people on the escalators because they're just standing there with guns. That's when I notice that they have on different uniforms from before. They're wearing vests with the word "ICE" on them—very appropriate because that's what's in their eyes and on their faces. I begin to be unable to stand still. My emotions are starting to crumble. My mind is falling apart and I don't care anymore. This is wrong and it is driving me crazy. I can't hold it together anymore. I start yelling at the "ICE" men. I am yelling out of control, "This is inhuman! We are human beings! Look at us, look at us!" They never budge. They never even look at me and I know they can hear me because I am standing right under them at the bottom of the escalators. They are trained to be that way. I understand that, but still. It's cold-blooded. How can they do this to us? How? The crowds start getting heated (no pun intended) and a serious outbreak of anger is about to happen. The Korean doctor comes out from time to time to advise which area we can go to for help if we need any particular services or if someone is looking for a family member. Then the lines start moving. Fifteen hours later. Oh, my God. Fifteen hours! We finally get to the door and I'm thinking, okay, I just want to get through this shit. And we get to the doors. The doors close. We have to wait. I honestly think that they are going on a damn lunch break, because people on the other side of the doors start disappearing. Finally they open the doors and we go through. Right before, we're told that if we have any weapons or drugs, to get rid of them. Weapons? Drugs? If I had any drugs I would have smoked them! Fuck! I can't believe that shit, man. It's like the Three Stooges are in charge of this whole thing.

So there's this woman with a uniform on that says Homeland Security. Young black woman, and she's (I learned this expression from a friend, Rhonsha Bryant, in Washington, D.C.) "grittin' on me." And she is being so rude. When they close the doors on us right before we're going to go through, I ask her why we are being treated so badly and so on. Yes, I'm yelling at her, but considering the circumstances, you know, I'm justified. So, she's staring at me with her arms folded like she wants to fight. So I say, what the fuck are you looking at me for? That's how some of us talk in New Orleans. I'm like, I don't know who I am, so I'm not gonna know who you are when I take you outside where nobody can see us, fuck you up, and go on about my business. Because what has gotten to me is I know she's doing her job. I respect that. But all she needs to say if she doesn't know what to say is, "I'm sorry for what y'all went through, good luck in the future." Something, anything! I mean, no compassion, no empathy, nothing. And that's all I'm asking for, that's all. And it doesn't matter that she's black like me, because I'm not looking for special treatment, just a little care or love. That's all.

So we get through this shit and end up sitting in the waiting area just as if we were waiting for our flight number to be called. Only this time the waiting area is dark and I know my mind is falling apart. We keep seeing everybody being called but us. And that is starting my "conspiracy meltdown." I think we're being kept there because of my outburst with the guard. Of course, I'm telling Ron this and, to be honest, he is rightfully tired. I have put him through absolute hell. While I'm sitting in the chair going crazy, this woman walks past me and says, "They ought to spray some Lysol in here." Y'all, I don't have the strength to do anything but look up at her. I gather up enough words that form in my mind and they are: No that bitch didn't! That's it. She does help me to realize how much I smell like shit and piss from being in that black water, and no bath for seven days.

I would like to personally thank her for making me want to die right there. But again, in that moment, I feel the spirit of God's Love. This is happening for a reason. Hold on Phyllis, hold on. Still, they do not call our names. They start putting people into groups, and it seems to me that the other groups have more than two people and the group that me and Ron are in only has us two. Oh, hell no! Something's wrong with this shit. Ron keeps trying to control me, but it's not working. I lose my intelligence again and ask this man with a uniform on if there is a restaurant open where we can buy some food. He says no, they themselves are waiting on food. I ask if we can buy something from them. He says, "No, we don't have anything, ma'am."

I feel like a homeless, stupid, dumb bum. No home, no place to call my own. Just lost. I go to the desk again and (I learned this one from the same friend) "flick on the woman." I start saying stuff like this is a conspiracy and they are leaving us out on purpose and I want to speak to someone in charge that is higher up than her. Oh, that's right, the city is flooded and I want your manager. Ron looks at me as if to say, Phyllis, sit your black ass down and shut up. But he doesn't. I personally think he wants to leave my crazy ass right there. You ever have someone in your family who "acts up" or has a mental problem, and when they do you look the other way like you don't know them? That's how Ron is doing my ass. He's like, just 'cause I'm sitting next to her don't mean I know her or that she's with me.

Saturday, September 3

Governor Blanco refuses to give up control of the state's national guard troops; twelve thousand are now on active duty.

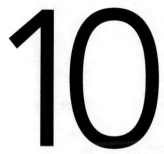**10** Okay, we get called. We are told that the next plane that comes in will be the one for us. A plane comes in, but doesn't land. We are told that there is some kind of problem. They won't tell us what type of problem, but that a replacement is being sent. All righty, now. Our plane arrives. We begin to board. I really can't remember much after that because at this point—and after all that I have gone through—I leave the real world and go into another place in my mind. I do remember falling asleep and dreaming that I was giving Ron a surprise birthday party and called the guy from the *Punk'd* show, Ashton Kutcher. This is where it gets weird. Just a little. So I'm dreaming that I contact the *Punk'd* show and tell them I want to play a joke on my husband, who swears the show will never get him. So I go through the motions of

talking to the show's staff, and I'm walking around whispering in their ears when I think Ron is not watching.

During this time we have landed in San Antonio, Texas, (I kind of remember seeing a sign) and are walking off the plane. I'm still sleeping (or so I think), so I'm actually acting out my dream in real time! Please pay close attention to this. In my mind I am dreaming. In the real world I am acting out what I am dreaming. Ron later told me that when we first got off of the plane I sat in a wheelchair and started to play around in it, laughing and whooping it up. He said I walked up to an armed guard and whispered something into his ear. The one guard let me go, but the next one felt I was a threat and twisted my arm behind me in order to restrain me. Ron walked over to the guard and explained to the guard that we'd been through a great deal and that I wasn't feeling well but would not cause any further disturbances. Ron then took my hand and walked me over to the restroom area and started explaining to me what other things I had been doing. He said I was walking up to complete strangers, whispering and laughing to them.

All of this he tells me when we are in line to go to an air force base. I break down, crying uncontrollably. I'm remembering my dream and here he is telling me I have been doing this in real life. I can't stop crying and fall to my knees. Ron comforts me, but I am pissed off at him. I mean, what in the hell did he think I was doing? He thought I was "just playing." So when that armed guard would have shot my ass, that would have been "just playing" too? I ask him why he didn't just smack me. He doesn't answer. So I leave it at that. Like I said, I have put Ron through hell and we were already going through hell. So, I forgive him, but I tell him don't ever do that again. I was in a bad place in my mind, and I needed for someone to pull me back.

Anyway, we go to this air force base and it's wide open, and there are all of these lights and hard-ass chairs. There are medical stations set up for any emergency medical needs that we might have. I want so badly to walk over and ask for a shot of Valium until it isn't even funny. I don't. We sit in those hard-ass chairs for hours, and then a bus comes to take us to a shelter. The bus is freezing. Now you'd think that this would be welcome but it isn't. All this cold air does is freeze my funk in midair, reminding me of just how bad I smell. Seven days of not bathing. Try smelling that and tell me whether you would want it frozen in time. I don't think so. We stay there until right before sunrise. Then by word of mouth we hear that there are people boarding buses to go to shelters. Only by word of mouth do we find this out. It is still dark while we are on the bus, but I can see apartments that look like military housing. I think we will be living in them but that would mean good treatment. Once again, shuttled off like cattle to the holding ground. We then arrive at this shelter called Kelly Air Force Base. There are tents set up all over the place. A large building sits in the middle of the grounds and there are Red Cross people everywhere. I remember this woman who has volunteered there walking up to me and putting her hand on my shoulder. I burst into tears. There is so much compassion and love in just that one touch that it opens up my heart. Somebody does care. I had to go all the way to San Antonio, Texas, to a shelter, but damn it, it is still in this world. And

I am a welcome mat for it. She advises us of what is available, telling us where the hot food is, and where to take a shower. In this fenced area there are mounds and mounds of clothing. I think nothing of it until I learn that it is donated clothing that people have sent for us. I start crying again. Reality sets in with the knowledge that we are poor and homeless, with nothing but the clothes on our backs. There is a place that we have to go and get shots just in case we got infections from being in that old, filthy, shitty-ass water. More lines. The place is crowded, very crowded. We have to stand in line for everything. The only thing that Ron has to stand in line for is a shower. All the rest I volunteer to go and get. Like I said before, I have put my husband through an emotional hell. I am trying to make up for all that I have done.

All of my life I've been a fighter. I mean, things in life would knock me down, but I always got up swinging. But, when Hurricane Katrina blew on me, I folded. I still, to this day, can't believe that I crumbled that badly. It wasn't so much Katrina, but how nobody came to help us, and when they did, so many people had already drowned, and most in their own homes.

I go to take a shower first, and let me tell you about hot water. Oh, hell yeah. This is getting better and better. Once again I'm in another world and this is good. I have little tiny bottles of shampoo and, get this, conditioner too! Oh, it is beautiful! Then I look down and see that I am standing on a wooden plank. Then I look around and see where I am and think about how someone else was just standing here and you can see some of the other people's bodies in the other showers. I burst into tears, but soft tears so nobody can hear me. My heart is so broken. My government, in my country, does not care about me, us: the Chocolate People. The tears fall down my face soft and quick, but fall hard on the wooden plank underneath my feet. And then I feel like a slave again. I mean, I know that I could never insult the history of my ancestors by comparing what I am going through with what they endured. But this has the "air of enslavement." That is how I feel. So I decide to try to wash that feeling away with that little tiny piece of soap. My skin is sore from the angry scrubbing I put my tired, black body through. I dry myself off, put on my paper shoes, throw my dirty drawers of eight days of wearing into the trash and step out into the open air.

Before Ron and I went to take our showers we went over to a large gated area in the back of the facilities and waded through donated clothing and I found a top and bottom set of medical scrubs that someone had donated to help us out, because most of us had no clothing but what was on our backs. I keep trying to remember all of the positive things I've told myself over the years to survive, and words from other people that helped me to survive in the years before this one. I recall saying over and over in my head the words of Dr. Maya Angelou: "When people show you who they are, believe them." This helps me to stop giving logic to what's happening to us. You know, like maybe they (the president of the United States, Condoleezza Rice, Chertoff, Ron Brown, FEMA) misunderstood the communication from our city officials. Maybe they thought the black bodies were just black water. I am coming back to my senses. Thank you, Dr.

Angelou, from the very walls of my heart, thank you. Once I step out in the open air, looking around and not seeing Ron, I start to panic. I don't want to be without him for a second. I ask around, and find some signs that tell me where the men's showers are. I don't go all the way to them, because I don't want to see anyone else's nakedness. I find a spot on some steps and wait.

We walk to find out what we have to do and where we have to go. There is a line to get sandwiches and chips and sodas. I tell Ron to go and find a table, and I'll get in line to get us something to eat. In this large room there are big-screen televisions showing what is going on back home. Hmph! Home. What's that? I leave Ron to go walk over and see what is going on. I can't believe my eyes. The water from the levees has practically covered our entire city! They don't show bodies but they are saying that tens of thousands are "feared dead, drowned." "Feared"? What in the fuck do they mean, "feared?" Had they come when we got hit, there would be no "feared." I just put my head down in shame and walk back to where Ron is sitting. We hear that there is a line where we can get toiletries such as lotion, bars of soap, deodorant, and such. I go in and get a bag of stuff for Ron and me. Then there is a line where we are supposed to go and get wrist bands for identification purposes. When I ask why we need wristbands I am told it's so they can identify us as residents of New Orleans. Whatever, man. Just give me the damn bracelet. The good thing is that I'd put my and Ron's identifications in a ziplock bag, so we'd have them with us the entire time. I kept the baggie inside of my underwear before we got to the shelter; now I hold them in my hand because I have no underwear to put on after taking a shower, and I damn sure am not putting on "donated drawers." The people who don't have identification are asked what their information is and it is recorded that way. And really and truly, at this point I don't give a damn about anyone else because I have enough of my own pain that I am dealing with, you know what I mean?

Then we have to find a place to sleep. So we walk around signing up for this and that; we even sign up for food stamps. They actually have an office where we can sign up for those. I guess they think that's what we were receiving before Katrina hit. Don't get me wrong; I don't see anything wrong with receiving food stamps if you need them, but I feel like they have this preconceived notion that we were all poor and destitute before Katrina. Oh well, food is food, no matter what you pay for it with.

We finally see somebody from back home, my aunt Sylvia. My mother's sister. She and her daughter, Kizzy, have found each other and ended up at the same shelter. So Ron and I stand there talking with Sylvia and then we see a few other people from our apartment complex. Then I see the guy from the New Orleans Airport: "The Evil One," the woman beater and child beater from my teenage years into young womanhood. He is working there! He passes by quickly and I say nothing because Ron is right next to me. I don't want anything to go any worse than now, so I say nothing. And besides, I have forgiven him through God for what he's done. I mention to my aunt Sylvia that I've seen him. She says to me, "Well you know, he's turned his life around and is into church, huh?" "Really," I say. "Interesting." So Ron leaves to go somewhere, and that dude passes by again. The reason I'm not giving his actual name is because he can write his own book and put his own name in it. Anyway, so he passes by again. I walk up to him and say, "You do know that I forgave you through Christ for what you did to me years ago." His response to me is, "Well you know, Phyllis, that was a long time ago." This is how he accepts my forgiveness. Oh well, the blood is washed off my hands, and my spirit flows joyfully and freely in that area of my life. But it was an interesting moment. When I told my aunt what he'd said, I can't quite remember what her response was but I'm sure it was meaningless because she said that she'd seen him on one of the riverboat steamships back in New Orleans and that he'd turned his life over to Christ and he had changed his life and was a different person. That's why it was meaningless to me, because had he "changed his life" he would have, in my opinion, accepted my offering of forgiveness with the love and ease of Christ. It is worth mentioning because it amazes me how true the Bible is when it speaks about forgiveness and how you begin to know the spirit by the spirit when God is living inside of you. No matter how many people try to break it apart for their personal reasons. To each his own, and free will is available to us all.

Ron comes back, and I tell him what just happened and of course the first question is, "Where is he?" This is an example to all of how easily and quickly that old devil will try and slip pains and hurtful things back into your life if you don't stay focused on the one and only God. That's all I'm saying. I tell Ron that I don't know where he is because I don't want our situation to get any worse than it already is and I change our conversation to something else. So we walk around the facilities and when we get to the sleeping area we know right away that this is not going to work because there are too many people, complete strangers, and it hadn't been medically confirmed yet but Ron suffers from sleep apnea, which makes you snore extremely loudly because of blocked nasal passageways. That crowd of people would mob us because of the noise Ron would make if we sleep in that room. And besides that, I do not feel safe sleeping in a room with hundreds of beds next to each other and no type of enclosure for privacy. We start thinking of a way to get the hell out of there. Thefts are already happening and we haven't even been there one night! It took about ten minutes after I plugged my aunt Sylvia's phone adapter in the wall for someone to steal it. Phone adapters or chargers are the hot item to steal, as a lot of people in their haste left theirs behind or couldn't get to them in the first place. We are finally able to reach my youngest sister, Lisa, in Brooklyn. She is able to wire us money that she's gotten from a friend.

Tuesday, September 6

Mayor Nagin orders a forced evacuation of New Orleans.

# 11

So now the question is, how do we find a motel close enough to the shelter that we can still access the facilities, and how do we find a Western Union? Through word of mouth we find out about a Motel 6 and get a taxi to take us there. By the time we get there Lisa has called the motel and reserved a room for us. Yes! We get into room 315 and there are two beds. By this time I want to sleep by myself, only because I know that Ron is right next to me and he's gone so long without sleep that his snoring could awaken the dead.

We bathe. And I know this may be too much information, but I cannot use the toilet. I'm serious. I cannot have a BM because it has been so long since we've had use of a restroom, even at my mom's apartment. I can't. When your mental state is messed up, it affects the entirety of your body. Now

I know. That same night we get, again by word of mouth, the news that FEMA has started paying for motel and hotel lodgings.

Our bodies collapse, but that is not real sleep. The next morning our hotel phone begins ringing off the hook, as people have been able to track us from the Red Cross information. I talk to my mom and sister Catherine and when she tells me what they went through after we were separated it nearly sets me back mentally. Catherine tells me that once they got on the helicopter, her, my mom, and Nicholas were dropped off on an interstate and had to climb a fence to get to the other side of it and wait for a bus to take them to Houston. When they arrived in Texas by Trailways bus they were left in front of the Houston Astrodome, which was being used as a shelter for the New Orleans "refugees," which is what we were being called at that time. So Catherine starts walking and flagging down a ride to take them to a hotel on the other side of the highway. A lady stops and gives them a ride to the hotel. Once they get there the asshole of a clerk tells them they have no vacancies. My mom pulls out her credit card, and like magic a room becomes available! How about that? They check in to the room, because I mean what are you gonna do? You have no other choice but to take the blatant discrimination because you have nowhere else to go. They go up to the room and bathe and as Catherine tells me, "Girl, I had to put on a pair of Momma drawers." This is something that we can laugh at, and do we laugh! They go downstairs to eat, and once settled, Catherine gets up to go and get some juice for Nicholas, and he grabs on to her leg, holding on for dear life, she says. It's as if he is afraid that she will not come back. Tears roll down her face as she looks down at her son, wondering what is going through his mind. As I said, Nicholas is autistic, so watching him hanging on to his mother's leg, and watching him eat like he'd never eaten before, is horrible. This is too much heartbreak. I mean, what is going on in this world that we grew up in and trusted?

Now the folks at the Motel 6 give us a "dinner." They invite all of the "refugees" and "evacuees" from New Orleans down for a dinner of spaghetti and meat sauce, salad, and soda. (Now, everybody in New Orleans knows that this is the cheapest dinner anyone can fix.) After we sit and talk for a while they give us brown bags with bologna (I'd forgotten how to spell that word, cause I hadn't used it in so long, but I remembered that Oscar Meyer song, remember that one?) sandwiches, chips, a soda, and a cookie. Oh, hell no! I feel so ashamed of myself. I mean people are feeding us! And cheaply, I might add. It may seem like I don't appreciate what they're doing, but I do. I'm rather taking a shot at how our government has left us in a position to have to make people feed us like a pack of animals. And damn right I want a steak and baked potato with that salad, and if it wouldn't be asking too much, a nice glass of Merlot. There, I said it.

It just seems like the world thinks of us as these poor, helpless misfits. And this is not true. I mean we aren't rich, but we work and pay our bills like every other "responsible American." I function, but it is like I am living in another world, and for the first time in my life I do not know what to do. This thing is really messing with my head. But God has a bigger plan. I just have to hold on.

Things become stranger and stranger. I guess through the Red Cross all types of people are able to contact us: both welcome and unwelcome. But out of desperation for some semblance of familiarity, we respond. I won't go into a who's who list. It is just really weird. A person who has not contacted Ron in years calls. This person has previously given Ron pure hell each time they spoke to one another. This is a very sensitive situation and I stay out of it. All of a sudden there is this big concern for his life and well-being. It still amazes me how people who treat you like shit try to slip back into your life for their own personal reasons and greed, like nothing ever happened. I wonder constantly how these people sleep each night. This world would be so much better if we stopped chasing and worshipping the almighty dollar. Money and greed have to do with this situation because people have been watching the news and have learned that we displaced evacuees are being given money from Red Cross and FEMA. Also, some people want to find out if people have maybe drowned so they can maybe cash in that way.

Ron has a son and a daughter who live in Dallas, Texas, with their mother and he had not heard from her until the hurricane, but she has chosen to call to see if he is still alive and wants to know what is going on with him and tells him that she has heard on the news that we are getting all of this money. She doesn't even think about the money being because we've lost everything. This area is very sensitive for Ron, so we can discuss further how much needs to be made known.

Some people don't care who they hurt to get it and who they are sacrificing to get it. I'm learning that the kids don't matter, just the anger at the other person. It's the children who suffer, and if you ask most kids, money doesn't matter. My own dad has never contacted me and I'm forty-three years old. I remember I wrote him a letter once telling him that money did not matter to me, and that all I wanted to do was to get to know him and where I came from. I just wanted to know who my dad was, that's all. I received a letter from him stating that what happened between him and my mother was between them, not understanding that I had no interest in what happened between the two of them. I wanted to know what that had to do with him and me. I never heard from him again. So on my next birthday I mailed him a birthday card with a dollar bill in it. The symbolism? A dollar bill can't buy much these days and money can't buy love.

Parents should stop letting money get in the way of a child's growth. I mean this across the board, and it doesn't matter who it is: family, friends, or complete strangers. We have women who refuse to let children know their other parent because of money. I mean, what is this teaching children? Think about it. In my opinion, I believe that since it takes two people to make a baby, then both parents should be held responsible for taking care of that child or children. It should not fall on the man (my observation is that men are more likely to be responsible for child support than women). I think in a case where the male parent is working and paying child support and that woman has about seven to eight hours a day, let's say, when they are in school, to do something, hey, why not get a job? Part time. Who enjoys sitting at home waiting on a check? Who really enjoys actually waiting on, depending on, someone to send them money? My mother got out there and did what she had to do, in spite of what my dad didn't do. She didn't chase him down hell-bent on making him pay. Or waiting each time he got a raise from the job that he went to every day, working hard, dirty work to run to court and ask for more money so she could lie on her lazy ass. My mother was never this type of woman. Never.

Don't get me wrong. I am not speaking about all women. Just the kinds who are guilty of what I am describing. If it doesn't apply to you then what would be your argument? You feel me? I'm sitting there listening to this stranger and I'm like, damn, I know Ron who is going through the exact same thing and I personally know this man. So, whether this stranger was being truthful or not, I know one who is truthful. So don't get all pissed off at me for saying what I know about personally. I just think that the children of this world would be better off and maybe, just maybe, have more of a chance in life if we didn't stop them from seeing their father because of money, especially when the man is at least paying the child support. And for the ones who don't, I think that they deserve a chance as well. Love is priceless. I believe if we would wake up with love, we would sleep better with love.

There's this guy I strike up a conversation with during our evacuation, and he starts to tell me about this woman that has kids by him. They split up a year ago and he's paying child support for his two children. He says the mother has sole custody of the children. He doesn't even have visitation rights. But each time he calls to spend time with the kids she intentionally starts an argument, changes her phone number, and eventually moves to another location. After several times of going through the same thing he's given up.

Still, he pays child support. Then the grandmother of the children began to help out with pictures and updates of the kids' progress. Then Hurricane Katrina hit. His ex contacted him through Red Cross. He said it was to see if he was still alive. She was worried about one or two things: that the child support would stop and whether or not she would get money if he'd died. I try to end the conversation, because I have enough of this kind of thing going on already. Get me? Still, I sit there and listen because maybe I'm supposed to be there and help just by listening. He continues telling me how this woman was acting all concerned at first. Then came the confirmation of the reason for the call.

She told him she'd heard on the news that Katrina evacuees would be getting all of this money, and even asked for him to send $600 because she wanted to buy their son five pairs of tennis shoes so he could wear a different pair every day. He sent cash, against his wife's opinion that a child that young did not need that many tennis shoes. His wife also offered that if he did send it, to do so in the form of money order. Rather, he sent $400 in cash. Then he sent her $300 in cash. Then he went to the bank and found his account was frozen by the courts because a phone call had been made to the child support office to investigate a large sum of money being deposited, and she wanted some of it.

He was confused. He'd forgotten about an argument they'd had, when he once told her "no." He grew tired of her taking advantage of his situation, so he put his foot down and she filed a complaint. He called the child support division and was told that because he had more money, they would need to reassess his income and increase his child support payments. He then called back and spoke with someone who actually wanted to do the right thing. This guy told him that all he had to do was send in his paperwork, showing this "increase" in income was a result of losses due to Hurricane Katrina, and that this money was legally not supposed to be touched by the child support system. Once the paperwork was received they removed the block on his account.

Soon after that, this man received the call that he was expecting from his ex because those funds could not be touched due to the nature of what they were for. The ex cussed him from top to bottom. She once again threatened to keep him from ever speaking with his children again. So he went back to sending cash. This opened the door to speak with his children, and what he called "sacrificial conversations" with her. He told me how often he cried, and that a man shouldn't have to cry that much. But because of fear and ignorance he complied with the demands of this woman. He simply did not know what else to do. The worst of it for him—and for me when he told me—was that once after he spoke with his kids and told them that he loved them, and they said they loved him too, she got on the phone and said, "They be lying, they just faking to get money."

This was one of the stories that I heard from other people after Hurricane Katrina. Some of the city and world's leaders were saying that Katrina meant cleansing; well, apparently some folks just like to plain stay dirty. We heard stories of babies and their mothers drowning in their own homes. My husband's friends were on a rooftop, and two houses down was an elderly couple. They had on life jackets and after the third day, that night the husband took off his life jacket and quietly slipped into the black waters, drowning himself because he thought nobody was going to come and save them.

You see, I was hit from the top by Hurricane Katrina, and hit from the bottom by the breach in the levees. There were some who received only wind damage and there were those who received complete damage like in the Ninth Ward, where entire homes were completely engulfed with water and some even moved off their foundations. Our apartment complex received approximately five feet of water on the first floor apartments. Our apartment was on the second floor and, although it did not receive flood water from the bottom, our roof in different parts of the apartment caved in from two apartments on the third floor above us where the rooftops blew off and came down on ours. The bottom part that I speak of is that the floodwaters from the breach in the levees stopped us from leaving the complex.

Back to Motel 6 in San Antonio. Ron and I begin to familiarize ourselves with the area as far as shopping places where we can purchase clothing and food and hygiene products. Most of everything that we need is within a mile. I usually walk to get the things that we need and the walking helps a great deal. Every now and again, you'll see someone at a store who is from New Orleans and sometimes you'll cry or just share a story or two and move on to getting your own life back in order. I have to be honest with you: I am sinking into depression. When you become unable to imagine into your future, that's when you know. We begin to hear, word of mouth, about FEMA paying for apartments and that FEMA would be paying for motels for an extended amount of time.

Once we hear this I honestly begin to feel a little hopeful that our government is finally going to help us to stop this suffering and displacement. My hope begins to build, but after what the people of New Orleans have already gone through, with our government holding back for so long, I am still a bit leery and cautious about trusting them.

Ron is worrying about his job and getting back to work. We have no transportation because his truck is under water back home. A beautiful family friend, Mr. Vernon Smith, lives in Houston, and he has begun helping everyone that he knows, as he is a native New Orleanian. He offers to rent us an automobile to get back and forth to the shelter, at Kelly USA. Kelly USA is an old airplane hanger that has been converted into a shelter for the evacuees of New Orleans. After several attempts, I am able to contact Ron's insurance at State Farm, and they supply us with a rental. Man! You have no idea of how hard it is to get an automobile because so many evacuees are renting cars. It makes for a long waiting list. During this time we've also heard that funds are being distributed to evacuees, and we

have to get to the center. We are able to access our checking account and take a cab to the site. The fare is almost $70. Then, when we get there, the line is blocks long. We have to stand in line outside, in the heat. Then, once inside, there are rows of chairs, and each time someone or a group of numbers is called we have to get up and move down—even though it takes about an hour or two for them to call the next group. It reminds me of playing musical chairs when I was a child. Only this time the prize is money to buy food and survive the abandonment.

The distribution site is this huge airplane warehouse. They have industrial fans blowing on us to keep us cool, and they hand out cold water. Some mothers have their babies with them and they cry and cry. You hear some people saying that you can get more money if you do this or that. Some are saying that they can't get anything. I try to tune out the voices, but return my awareness to the present because scary voices came to my mind again, talking about drowning, starving to death. I start to remember the black water lapping against the side of the apartment when we were back in the complex, the woman calling for help, and the black water calling for me to come into it. So I choose to be in the moment with living voices. They are irritating, but safer.

After several hours of this madness, we are given a check. A check! Okay, where in the hell are we going to cash a check? Oh, the system has a solution. We go to the bank and they cash it for us. Half the damn people there lost their identifications in the storm. Oh, but the bank has a solution: if you want your check cashed, you have to open an account with them and agree to a fee. This is only the beginning of what will turn out to be an absolute exploitation of a people.

Well, we have our driver's licenses and identifications. So we are good. We take the ride in the cab back to the motel. I know the economy in San Antonio has shot through the roof, because there are cabs lined up around the block. They know we have no transportation, and they take every advantage of the fact. I wonder now if they put that place so far away from the shelter so that the cab companies could make all of that money from us? Makes one wonder, doesn't it? Ron used to always tell me that I don't trust people enough. I always told Ron that he trusts people too much. It's not that I don't trust people initially. When I first meet somebody, I always give them the benefit of the doubt. It's on that person whether they prove me wrong.

So many things happened during and after Hurricane Katrina that it would take volumes of books to write about it. But it is time for people, all people, especially those who have been on the short end of the stick for years, to open their eyes and wake the hell up. That's all I'll say on that one. WAKE UP! So anyway, whew, this is exhausting reliving all of these memories. I swear, I will never bring myself through that again.

I don't care who stays, I know that I am leaving. That said, the Motel 6 is nice in comparison to living on the grass and ground. The people who manage the motel and their family members who provide a "welcoming luncheon" for the evacuees residing in the motel are not bad and they help me to survive. There is a family living down on the first floor and Ron knows the husband. They have found an apartment across the highway and are kind enough to give us their microwave, or was it a mini refrigerator? I can't remember. I mean we have microwave shrimp, microwave eggs, microwave bacon, even microwave rice. There is nowhere to go but back and forth to the shelter each time we hear that they are giving something away to the "refugees."

I mean, I know a lot of human rights groups are angry about the use of that term, and I was for a minute. But actually, it helps me to laugh because I think of the singing group, the Fugees, with Lauryn Hill. I kind of want to dance, you know? We do what we have to do in the motel and as Ron continues to try reaching his place of employment, I just sit by and take in all of the stories that people are telling.

Ron finally gets in touch with his job, and they want him to come back immediately. So we rent an automobile. It is so small that I think we are on our way to the circus. You've seen them. The little car filled with all those clowns. Yet, this shit seems real because we are in a great sense being "clowned." On our way out we stop at a Wal-Mart and buy things like flashlights, batteries, inflatable beds, air pumps, and blankets. I think we even buy tents. Now mind you, we do not know where we are going to live.

Once we get into town, we stop at a relative's house in what we call "the country." We are invited to stay the night. You know, take a shower, and have a nice clean bed to sleep in. Well, the next day we are taken on an apartment hunt. I mean, I have never in my life gone through an entire apartment-finding book and found nothing. And everybody in New Orleans knows exactly what I mean. There is nothing available. Nothing. So we call and call another relative and finally, after the calls keep dropping we just drive there.

Now the first spot we stay is in Gramercy, Louisiana with Ron's sister, Lori, and her fiancé Kevin. We sleep there for one night and it's fun, because there are children there and that area has not been affected, at least not to my knowledge, by Hurricane Katrina and it is a very large home with about four or five bedrooms and they make room for us. The next day Ron and I go in search of an apartment but everything is completely sold out. So Ron and I and Lori drive over to the house of another relative of his, Marcia and Mark Tureaud in Gonzales, Louisiana, and we live there for about three months. It is also very nice and we are treated as family there as well. The first place was actually closer to his job, but this current place is where we live and survive. Ron is back working and has to drive eighty miles to work and eighty back, and this is killing him. Each time I express to Ron my worry about his driving like this, all he keeps saying is that we have to get all of what we owned all over again. We have lost everything and we have to buy it again. He has to take care of his kids who live out of town with their mother. We never live off of anyone for nothing. We pay our way, and we have no problems with doing so. Finally, after those wonderful months, Ron receives a phone call saying that if we want to come back to the first spot, we will be very welcome.

We go back. During our stay there I get a phone call from my oldest sister, Gina. She tells me that she has interviewed with some people who work for Spike Lee, and that they are thinking about doing a documentary about the levees breaking and all. She asks me if it would be okay to give one lady, Judy Aley, my phone number because she has told her that I have a story to tell. Gina explains to me how this type of thing goes, you know: questions and answers, and stay true and to the point. I am nervous as hell, but I tell Gina, "Okay, give her my number." So Judy calls, and right from the start, she is so nice. Her voice is like if you go to a therapist and you lie on a couch, that kind of voice. Very therapeutic. So we talk, and she explains what we will do. She asks me what I've gone through and before I am even close to being done she stops me and says she wants to record what I am saying. I'm cool with this. So I start my story and all the time I'm talking, in between she's like, "Oh, my God. Oh, dear." Just being so empathetic about my story, and this is what makes it better and better. It's like I am in therapy and she is my counselor. She is one of the most beautiful people that I have ever met in my life and I mean this. So when I finish, I can tell I have nearly wiped her out.

She gives me words of encouragement and compassion, and we talk some more and then I ask her, "What happens now?" She says that she'll give the recording to Spike, and if he wants my story told, it will be. I'm paraphrasing, but that is basically it. She says I will receive a call to go forward if necessary. I do receive a call, and interview again with Judy and Butch Robinson, who is also another person that I think is one of the coolest brothers to meet. I mean, the love is just there. They don't make you feel stupid for staying or anything. They just feel so much love for our city that you can feel it. You can feel that they are also pissed off at the slow response to our situation. I have gotten my girlfriend Shera Burrell-Young to come with me. And they interview her as well. After we finish, they take us to lunch and it seems like the old New Orleans, until the waiter shows up to take our order and he has blue hands. Yes, blue hands. So after he takes our order and walks away, I ask if I was the only one who noticed that the dude had blue fucking hands. Everybody else has noticed too. When he returns I say, politely, "Excuse me, but why are your hands blue?" He explains that he was working on rebuilding his home and working here as well. The food is suddenly not worth eating because, first of all, the red beans taste like someone cooked them in an hour's time and anyone from New Orleans knows that a good pot of red beans takes at least two to three hours! Then his hands are blue and he doesn't have any gloves on or anything to try and cover them up. So I'm thinking, okay, I survived that damn hurricane and now he's about to kill me with lead or paint poisoning.

We finish up at the restaurant and I ask, "What next?" Judy and Butch say I will be getting a call soon to speak with Spike. My damn nerves are so bad it cannot be explained, but it does give me something else to think about. So, I get the call that I'm to meet the man who tells his story and sticks to it, Mr. Spike Lee. A car comes to pick me and Shera up from the hotel where she and her family are living, post-Katrina. We get to the Louis Armstrong Airport, and my world starts to crumble. This is where we were for those fifteen hours I talked about before. So we meet the crew, and everyone's nice, and I immediately light a smoke. Shera is not fully getting what's going on inside of my body, so

I just keep talking and trying to calm myself down. A few minutes later, a limousine pulls up and although I can't see who it is, I know.

We continue to talk and walk around, Shera and me. Then another nice person comes to get us—Bo-Deeni is his name—and he is cool, and friendly. He explains that Spike is here, and we are to go inside of the airport and wait to meet him. I'm freaking. Not about meeting Spike, but about going back into this airport. This is my first time back since the storm. It's been about three months since then. We go in and are asked to have a seat in these chairs at the bottom of the escalators, right where the ICE unit had been standing. Then I look over, and there it is, the exact same spot where Ron and I were standing all of those hours. Tears come to my eyes, and just as I am about to go deep into the memory of it, someone comes and gets us to go up the escalators to meet Spike. I walk so fast to get up the escalators and away from that spot that I forget my purse, so I have to go back down the damn escalator.

I tell Shera about my emotions running high, and we talk a little until the guy comes out and escorts us into a room to meet Spike. His vibe is very comfortable and he speaks very low. His air of confidence gives me a major boost, and I begin to relax. We talk for a minute as he explains what is to happen. Okay, cool. Then I ask him if I can ask him two questions. He says sure. I ask, "How are you going to portray my people, and can I cuss?" He says he wants the world to see what the news was not showing and yes, I can cuss. "Just be yourself and tell your story." And that's what I do. But it's hard telling my story. It hurts a whole lot, just like it's hurting me now to write this. So we finish up that part of the filming. He tells me that they may want to film me again. And I am okay with that. But let me say this: there is a part in the documentary where I'm talking about the phone call to the operator where I ask her to connect me to 911, and I put my finger up because the tears are about to begin falling. I put the finger up to stop them, and when I do this, Mr. Lee says, "Take your time, just take your time." You can't hear him say this on the documentary, but I can, and he is so serious, and that's when I know that he cares about not just me but us, the people: his people. So then we go downstairs, and he interviews Shera. Then he thanks us and the car is coming for us, but I tell them never mind because I called for Ron to come and get us. Ron gets there and I call Spike over to meet Ron. They shake hands and share a few words and we leave. But not before Spike tells me that they are interviewing the director of the airport and he's saying there was "no incident, and all was well." I go the fuck off, and Spike is like, "Now, now, let the man have his say," and he is right. But I still wanted to kick his . . . well, let me move on. So we leave and go back to "the country." We return to Ron's sister and fiancé's home in Gramercy, Louisiana. Not the Tureauds. This is better for Ron, because it is even closer to his job. Then we get word from Warner Leblanc, Ron's eldest brother, that a hotel room is available through a family friend named Melvin.

Melvin is a contractor and has some workers in town. That particular hotel is only (seemingly) making rooms available to business owners and then these employers are able to provide shelter to their workers. Warner and Melvin work together, and this is how Melvin has found out Ron's situation—the travel time to his job and it being too damn far to drive. The distance is killing my husband, and something needs to be done. After Warner explains to Melvin what the situation is, hell, Melvin offers us his room, as he is traveling for long periods of time out of town, I think to New York or somewhere. This is what I mean when I tell my people, and all people, to wake up. If and when it is possible, help others, as you never know when you may need help.

I believe that true blessings come from the heart, when you do something for someone with no strings attached or looking for how it will benefit yourself. Character is something that a lot of people think they have but don't. They have no clue. I wanted to put a cuss word in front of clue, but the point can be made without it. Hurricane Katrina and the aftermath showed what a lot of people's character was. Again, I said it before and I'll say it again, the word Katrina should mean "exposure" because that's what she did. She exposed a lot of what's wrong in this world and also a lot of what's right. If people were stealing before Katrina, and then stole after Katrina, why are we surprised? I mean, it didn't surprise me; it only saddened me that some people will never change, no matter how much tragedy falls upon them, around them, and right in front of their faces.

I have since vowed to seriously work to stop trying to understand why people do the bad things they do, and focus on how I can serve people to the best of my ability with love, compassion, empathy, and kindness.

We get the information for the hotel, go there and check

in. I know this may sound crazy to those whose home is not in New Orleans, but like Dr. Michael Eric Dyson says in his book, *Come Hell or High Water*. I am so freaking glad to be home, it's like crazy as hell how I feel. Amid all of the destruction that has broken my heart into two pieces, I am glad to be home. I mean, it's true when they say, "Home is where the heart is." And my heart is in New Orleans.

The entire hotel is filled with "Katrina Evacuees." Ron continues to work a schedule that leaves me feeling so lonely, I have to remember we're married. I mean I know that I am married but he is gone so long that my feelings of surviving alone are becoming like second nature. We talk every day, several times a day, but it just isn't the same. The only time I leave the room is to get food, which I have to eat right away, because the miniature refrigerator we purchased has blown a fuse. I asked the hotel's engineering department several times to repair it. But, I kind of got the message that they will not be complying with my request. I mean, we are "FEMA people." If you're from anywhere in Louisiana, particularly New Orleans, you know exactly what I mean.

I start mentally coming around to where I am. This is my

131

city, no matter that there are those who try to make me feel that I don't belong here, and am no longer wanted here. I dig into what I call my "customer service skills." I begin speaking to the hotel's personnel in a manner of pleasing them, and the shit is working. I am able to convince all but one.

I'm lying in bed watching the three channels that we have been provided. When we first checked in we had cable access but soon that has changed. When I inquire at the front desk about the channels being reduced, I am told that the hotel is "experiencing technical difficulties." These "technical difficulties" will last the entirety of our stay there.

Then I have what I call "the Mouse Incident." When I first see the thing, I think I am experiencing some type of hallucination. So I continue to watch television. Then I see it again. So I politely call the front desk, explaining that I need someone to get a mouse out of my room. You see, I actually consider myself a guest of the hotel and assume that hotel staff will give us service, and attention to this problem. Wrong. The clerk's response is, "I'm not surprised, as people are leaving bags of trash in the hallways. I'll let engineering know about it, and someone should be up there tomorrow."

Tomorrow? What in the hell do you mean, tomorrow? She advises me that the engineer has gone home for the evening, and that is the best that she can do. So I call Ron at work, and tell him what's going on, like he could actually leave work and come and kill the damn thing. Meanwhile, I'm sitting on the bed, hunched up in the corner, watching for the damn mouse. I see him running across the floor into the area where our suitcases are and I decide that they will be thrown away. Because I know damn well I am not touching those bags again.

I call the front desk again, but that proves unfruitful and I just sort of give up, at least for the night. The next morning, bright and early, I call the front desk at 5:00 AM and speak with the security guard. He is the front desk personnel until the actual shift comes in at 9:00 AM. I am not falling asleep risking the chance of a mouse crawling into bed with me. So after speaking with security and explaining to him how pissed off I am at the hotel for not treating me with hospitality, I hang up. Finally, the day shift arrives and I ask again for someone to come to my room and kill the damn mouse. The "engineer" says that he will look into it for me, but he never comes back. I guess since FEMA is paying for the rooms we aren't deemed as important as actual guests. So I am left to fend for myself against that damn mouse! It is as if they think that I am somehow from an environment that comes with mice. I don't know, but I am not giving up. Finally a knock on the door, and in comes engineering, this middle-aged black guy who has this air about him like he is glad to finally be able to treat some guests badly. Or maybe he has been picked on as a child, and this is a chance for "catch back." I don't know. He looks at me and says the damndest thing. He says that he can tell that the mouse has come in from a hole in the wall. Well, no shit, Mr. Sherlock Holmes! Hell no, he doesn't say a damn thing about closing up the hole so I take my suitcase and block the hole with that and I don't see the mouse again. They probably think like the president's mother—that we come from poverty anyway and a mouse is something that we are used to. BULLSHIT!

He is no help, but the next day housekeeping comes while I'm out and vacuums up the area where the mouse was chewing through the wall. There are other indications that we, as "FEMA people," are not considered guests: there are no curtains on any of the windows. I have to take a shower with the lights out so nobody can see me from the gas station across the street. The light switch doesn't work in the bathroom after a while anyway, and the wires are hanging out of the wall. We don't have comforters on the bed, just those fleece blankets that are itchy, like fleas are crawling on you while you sleep. Then, eventually, we have no phone service. When I call down to the front desk to ask about the phone being off they say they are having problems with people making long-distance calls and not paying for them. I tell her that I only want to use the phone for local calls, because I have my cell phone for long-distance calls. I am told that I have to come to the front desk and put down a deposit. Even after I do this the phones have "technical difficulties" for the duration of our stay.

We make do with what we have. I mean, after all, this is better than sleeping on grass, concrete, and anywhere else you could. FEMA is paying a special increased rate for these rooms. I know because I see what their room rates were before the storm, and then what the newspapers say FEMA is paying for "hosting" evacuees.

I only go out of the room on this balcony area inside the hotel to occasionally get fresh air, or, for food. One day I see Mr. Evil, the abusive man from my past. He tries to talk to me, saying that "maybe God sent me to talk to you." I tell him that this is impossible and he asks me, "How do you know that?" I say, "Because you had to ask." And walk away. This man did bad things to teenagers back in the days. He beat them, raped them, forced them into prostitution or tried to, and introduced them to drugs. He even beat one young woman with a wire hanger after she refused to let him put her on the streets to sell her body. He brainwashed them, and beat fear into them. Now I am one to believe that some people can change. But I'm also smart enough to know that some won't. He is one of those who won't. He is in a new car with a shady-looking white man. The white man has never looked at me while he tried to talk to me. Never. I know they are up to something and it is no good. I walk away from him, thanking God for allowing me to see him for the evil person that he was and is.

We finally get word that a trailer will be delivered for us on my sister Catherine's property. FEMA delivers our trailer to the property the next day. But it takes months for the electricity to be turned on, and for us to be able to live in it. So we continue to move from one hotel to the next because we are evicted from one hotel, then another. We are being evicted because FEMA continues to try and say that we evacuees should be able to find our own place to live, so every month or so they evict us and one of the civil rights groups, mostly Reverend Al Sharpton or ACORN files a lawsuit and FEMA reinstates the payments to the hotels for us to live in. FEMA gives us another extension code, and we are able to live in the hotel for a short while and then get evicted again. This goes on for months.

Finally, the electricity is connected. I am so scared that they have not done it correctly that I don't want to sleep in the trailer, because I think it will catch fire. Ron finally convinces me that everything is okay. Hmmm. Where have I heard that before?

Anyway, I listen to him. It is stressful having him go back to work for the fourteen days and be off for only two weekends per month. I am seeing my husband four days out of the month. Otherwise, I am alone to face what comes: thunderstorms. Oh, my God. I honestly think that I'm going to have a heart attack. I call Shera and ask her to come and pick me up, so that I will at least have some company until the storms pass. She and her family have two trailers on her property. So she comes and picks me up and drops me back when it is all over. I mean, they are predicting thunderstorms with a chance of a tornado three to four times a week. I don't think I can take this anymore. And I am getting tired of this running. It seems like nobody understands just how hard this is for me either, because the storms don't affect others like they do me and I know that most people around me do not understand just how deeply and emotionally I am affected. People who left before the storm hit the city and the people like us who stayed were affected differently and I understand this completely.

Spike Lee calls, and says they want to interview me again. This time it will be at the voting polls. The race for mayor is on. Mayor C. Ray Nagin is running for reelection! There are so many people running for mayor that I almost throw my own hat in the ring. But I don't, of course. I meet the film crew over at the voting polls on Chef Highway. The shoot goes well. I express my viewpoints: my thoughts of suicide and other things. I have no problem sharing what's going on inside and around me, because I feel like I'm not doing it just for my own sake. I am doing it for others too. I didn't know for sure then that I was helping anybody else, but I know now.

A couple of people have a problem with me talking about having thoughts of suicide during the hurricane as well as my cussing, but what they don't understand is me. I am who I am and the only one that can judge me is The One, God Almighty. Nobody comes to sleep on my sofa in this trailer, to comfort me from fear of the storms. Nobody calls and asks how I am doing except my momma, Mrs. Clovina Rita McCoy, my sister Mrs. Catherine Montana-Gordon, my sister Ms. Cheryl Ann Montana, my other sister, Ms. Lisa Montana, Judy Aley, Spike Lee, and my husband Ron, who has to put up with me until "death do us part." These people ask me how I am doing. These people call when they see on the Weather Channel that a thunderstorm is coming this way. Like I said, my girl Shera comes and picks me up on several occasions, and I appreciate that. She even tries to take me to a doctor's appointment, but it doesn't work out too well because she takes me to the wrong clinic. Once she gets her washer and dryer hooked up in her home she lets me do my laundry as well. She is going through the homeowner's version of the post-Katrina experience, as most of her home was filled with water. I think it took in about six or seven feet of water in eastern New Orleans. During the filming at the voting polls, I am asked by Spike who I voted for, and I tell him Mayor C. Ray Nagin. My choice for doing this is simple: there are too many people hungry for that seat. I mean, too many. I think it is because some of them know that there will be a lot of money coming into the city, and some of them want to get their hands on it. I have since forgiven New Orleans city officials for what they did or didn't do for us. I have to, or else I'll be stuck in Hurricane Katrina and the levees breaching for the rest of my life.

I don't trust the leaders and the politicians anymore, and their word means nothing to me. They lied, they took too long to get help for us, and people died because of this. This is what I saw. So we finish up with the filming, and again Spike Lee and the crew are very supportive of our still going strong by staying in the FEMA trailer, even though my fear of thunderstorms is getting worse and worse. I mean, one time Ron comes home from work, and I am sitting on the floor in the corner between the refrigerator and the bathroom door. I'm so distraught after a thunderstorm that even Ron being there does no good. He just sits on the sofa and then asks me to come and sit next to him. I refuse. I explain to him that I have to wait until I feel comfortable enough to move. After about twenty minutes, I move and sit next to him on the sofa. As soon as I hear thunder rolling I go right back to my "safe spot." This happens so often that I think that I will die from fear.

What is happening to my life? I keep remembering what I went through during the storm, and I don't know how to control these feelings. I pray but the more I pray on this fear, the more it comes. So I keep on praying, I keep on fighting, not realizing this battle is not mine to fight. How can I stop weather? Do you know that sometimes I sit my silly self down and sing that childhood song, "Rain, rain, go away, come again another day"? Yes, I do that.

I buy coloring books and a set of jacks. Once I know weather will be bad I get my coloring books and crayons, put these crane operator earplugs in my ears that I asked Ron to get from his job for me, and color. As long as the sound of the storm is not loud enough for me to hear, I am a little bit better. So I get through it, man, and I'm still going through it. I'm not as bad as I used to be; in fact I'm much better. Maybe that's because as I'm writing this, it's cold and thunderstorms are fewer, but that's okay. This time gives me the chance to get closer to God and become stronger. Laugh at me, talk about me, and let me tell you, it does not matter, because I deal with this without you. Maybe I'll help someone who's going through the same thing or similar. I'm just telling my experience.

# 14

Finally, Spike's people call and say they want to do an interview and filming at the trailer. I agree, but I'm getting tired. It's like I keep reliving this thing each time I talk to them, but at the same time, it's like free therapy. I ain't lying, this is working for me. But it is rough, especially with cameras focused on me, and all of these people watching. Mr. Lee makes it as easy as he can for me and so do his people. He asks the questions and I answer them. There is no script or practice—nothing like that. What you see on the documentary is as real as it gets.

The night before they come to the trailer, I speak with Butch Robinson, who gives me the time of arrival and such, and as soon as I get off of the phone with him this poem comes to my mind. I call the poem "Not Just the Levees

Broke." So the next day, while they are setting up the cameras, I tell Spike that I have written a poem, and ask him to give me his opinion. He glances over it really quickly and says, "Read it."

NOT JUST LEVEES

Not just the levees broke

The spirit broke, my spirit

The families broke apart (I want my momma, my sister, and my nephew back home)

The auction block broke from so many African-American bodies

The sense of direction was broken because of the darkness

There was light from time to time, but they broke away and left us

My being together broke when I fell apart

The smell broke away from my skin when I came out of the waters

The waters that came and stood still, with the bodies of my people, the dogs, shit and piss, rats, snakes and "heard of" alligators

The broken smiles, the broken minds, the broken lives

And you know something? You wanna know something? Out of all of this brokenness, I have begun to mend. With God, my deep, deep commitment to infinite strength and to never give up. I am mending. I am coming back. God willing, for a long, long time. So, when you see the waters. When you see the levees breaking.

Know what they really broke along with them . . .

Spike had no idea before that I wrote poetry, and really he wasn't supposed to, because he was here for the stories of survivors in New Orleans. I think to myself, damn this must be good if he's agreeing to have me read it. I actually only want his opinion on it, honestly. I read it twice. What appears on the documentary is from the first take. The second time I stumble on a word or something. He asks me to look at the camera when I read it, but I can't. You would never hear the words, because I would be a crying fool. Especially when I say the part about wanting my momma, my sister, and my nephew back home. That is my heart you are hearing. I know it's words, but to everyone who hears that poem, you are hearing my heart. After we finish up filming and we're sitting outside, I ask Spike if this is the last time that they will film me. He says, "Yes, why?" I say, "Because I'm tired of doing this." He says, "Yes, this is the last one, but let me warn you. When you see your story along with the stories of the others, I suggest you get ready. It is going to be rough."

I'm glad he gave me that "heads up," but it does me no good when I actually see *When the Levees Broke*. I get to the premiere, and there's this red carpet deal going on, and I'm like thinking, I'm just going in with my access pass to see the documentary. Baaaaaaaaby. I get in the place, and cameras start flashing, people are calling my name to turn this way, turn that way. "Phyllis, over here! Phyllis, can I get an interview? Phyllis, let me get a shot of the back of the shirt, the front of the shirt." Oh, it is wild. Here I go again: therapy. It's wonderful, and Spike did tell me that I was going to get a lot of attention from those who see it before we do. But I'm like, "Stop lying, you gotta be kidding." Oh, but he was not lying, and even to this day people are still coming up to me thanking me and telling me how proud they are of me, and that I said what they wanted to say. Yes, they are my therapy too. These people have helped me to survive. That is what we are about here in New Orleans, love. Especially my people in New Orleans East. This is where Ron and me are living, and everywhere I go people come up to me and recognize me. Some ask for autographs, and I tell them to stop playing. But some are very serious and I have to give them the autograph. It's a lot of fun, and it's healing because we are back and we are here to stay.

But not all is well in New Orleans. It breaks my heart to see my young black brothers killing each other, because it's really not necessary. Every day I'm looking at the news and there is a murder or two or three and they are all African-American males. It's happening so much that the African-American community is seemingly becoming numb to it. I don't have any children, but I know that when I was a child all I wanted from my mother was love and I got it. I got it in the form of soup and a grilled cheese sandwich when I had the mumps. I got it in the form of an ass whipping if I did something really bad. I got it in the form of discipline, respect, and obedience. Mothers, your sons need to know that you love them. It's not okay that taking a life has become so easy for so many young brothers. It's not okay when your son comes home with thousands of dollars, expensive clothing, and cars. Education is supposed to start at home from you. If you did drugs, tell them what it leads to and how you yourself stopped and why.

Television is not the place to leave your children alone. Even on regular channels the commercials are sexually explicit and violent. I am pleading and begging for the lives of our young black males to last longer than twenty-one and twenty-two years. At the same time, I don't live with these young brothers and I don't know if they've gone to bed hungry or had no clothes or were abused verbally or emotionally. So I can't walk up to and will not walk up to a drug dealer and ask him to stop because I don't know his hurt that got him to that point. I do have my own little "save-a-young-brother-network" going. Each chance that I get, when someone comes up to me and I think that they are "doing their thing," I drop positive words and a couple of things that I've been through. Again, I ain't the police and I damn sure am not going to act like it. I'm 504 not Five-O. My heart cries for them because just talking to a lot of young brothers I see that the intelligence and brilliance are there, they're right fucking there and in a great many of the cases the parents are failing the children. Not all, but a great deal. It's not okay that we are losing a big piece of our great African heritage. It's not okay. If I ever get to a point in my life where I am financially rich I am going to build those parks and community centers and not just pop up on Thanksgiving handing out turkeys or Christmas handing out a red or green box. I give every chance I get and I ain't even close to being where some others who don't give back are. Something as simple as when I go through the drive-thru at McDonald's I pay for the person behind me. Just to make someone's day, shit like that, you know what I mean? I do other things and they are unexpected and I am not going to sit here and tell you, but I will tell you that I know how to give the love. I love my race and the human race as well; I just pray that we as a race can claim our prize in this season of life and realize that it's not in the form of a gun, the death of another brother, or a jail cell.

The thing is, I cannot possibly judge them because I don't know what kind of life they grew up in, and what their daily struggles are either.

I want to tell them, even though I don't know them, that I love them. You don't have to know a person to love them. I'd tell them that if your life has you looking over your shoulder every minute, it has got to be rough. If your life has you on the run, and you can't trust in anyone, not even your own family or so-called friends, your life must be rough. Again, Katrina and exposure go hand in hand. The hurricane blew in and opened up a lot of what was hidden from the world: the crime, the corruption, the homeless people, the racism, the slow response from our government, and the whole rack of other shit that could happen in any city, state, or neighborhood. A lot of "spiritual leaders" say Katrina means "cleansing." I say it means Kicked Ass Today Revealing Inside Names Afterward. I could think of a few more from the letters of Katrina but that ought to do it.

Like I say, I don't have children, but I was a child once. I am a middle child in my family. I have two older sisters: Gina and Catherine. I have two younger sisters: Cheryl Ann and Lisa. And I have a brother, Thomas, who is the youngest of all of us. My siblings and I are very close. We have our run-ins every now and again, but we are always cool. We all have different issues and viewpoints, but try to respect each other. Those among us who take longer to muster up the respect simply take longer, that's all.

My thinking right after Hurricane Katrina was that our city would keep working together and kind of put aside our racial differences and class differences, but it seems to me that we are right back where we started. Some people have made positive changes in their lives while others have either stayed the same or become worse. Racism is still an issue and so is black-on-black racism within our community. We have certain political leaders talking out of both sides of their mouths. For example, these politicians will get on television or speak at rallies for justice and say that they want all people from New Orleans to come home. Then you read in the New Orleans *Times-Picayune* that those same politicians are trying to block low-income apartments from being rebuilt. They are phony-ass liars and just like Hurricane Katrina, put everyone on the same level of class and status. When all our asses were homeless and couldn't come back home we sang like a choir. Now we got a lot of folks wanting to do solos and so on and so on. But everyone has a right to choose what they want or don't want in their lives and opinions. I just thought that things could and would be better, but not too much has changed. And yet a lot has: exposure and Katrina.

After the premiere and all of the "local stardom," I still come back to my trailer and the storms still come. There has to be a time to deal with my fear, and I take steps to do just that. My relationship with God has gotten much stronger. The heart that was broken by people during and after Katrina is still healing.

During the times when I experience the fear I often think about seeing a doctor about it, but want to try and do it on my own. Me and God, that is my plan. But you see, even that is wrong, it is supposed to be God and me. You feel me? So while I'm trying to figure this part out, I start getting these "dizzy spells." I think nothing of it, just maybe some stress. It'll pass.

I begin to think about seeing someone, maybe a counselor, regarding my thoughts and feelings and those damn anxiety and panic attacks. So FEMA and other city, state, and government agencies list these phone numbers that you can call to speak with someone about hurricane-related issues. But here's the rub, if you will: when you call the numbers they ask you for your zip code and then they refer you to a hospital that is either relocated to another city or was completely destroyed by Hurricane Katrina. At least this is my experience. I try a few more places but give up because it is causing more anxiety for me to try to find someone to talk to about anxiety. Shit! At any rate, I resolve to try Xanax pills for six months to one year, or at least until we move out of the trailer. That's working out fine for me.

Now, I have been driving for about just two months.

Nicholas Tyler Gordon, my nephew! Hurricane Katrina survivor! Nicholas is eleven years old and attends Humble Middle School. He is in the sixth grade and attends life skills class for autistic students. To know him is to love him. He is the son of my sister Catherine Montana-Gordon and her late husband, Helmon Michael Gordon Jr.

My mother, Mrs. Clovina Rita McCoy, polishing her nails at home in Houston, Texas. She lives with Catherine.

Phyllis and Louisiana national guard sergeant Morris Patterson.
His unit patrolled the New Orleans East area, assisting
the New Orleans Police Department. The area was very
unpopulated at the time of this picture.

Phyllis and Private Walls of the Louisiana national guard
keeping the city of New Orleans safe! I had to convince
both Sergeant Morris Patterson and Private Walls to take
these pictures and to smile. They were so "serious."

Phyllis Montana-Leblanc and puppy, Brooklyn (my baby of peace)! And my cousin Daryl Montana, Big Chief of the Mardi Gras Indians, the Yellow Pocahontas tribe. This day is called "Super Sunday," when all the "tribes" come out and show their art of handmade "suits."

TOP Phyllis and Ron's living room. Picture taken from front door entrance by Ron. The weight of the water and other rooftops crashing onto ours knocked the ceiling open.

BOTTOM Phyllis and Ron's living room after Hurricane Katrina. Ron took a picture of the mold and mildew along the ceiling and walls where the "water bubbles" once were. Picture taken from outside of kitchen area.

Phyllis and Ron's living and dining area seen from front door. The entire area was completely drenched from open ceilings. This looks like a "graveyard" that Katrina dug but God said different!

Phyllis and Ron's bathroom after Katrina gave it a bath!
I had just redecorated my bathroom in the color of gold!

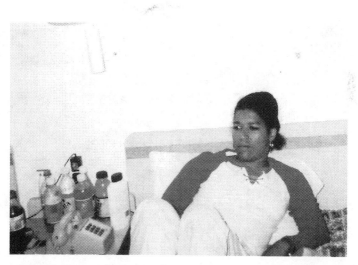

Phyllis at Motel 6 in San Antonio, Texas, the first week of
September 2005. The clothes I have on were donated by my sister
Lisa Montana and the loving people of Brooklyn, New York!!

These are the steps that Ron and I ran to when we were stuck on the other side of the apartment complex during Hurricane Katrina. It still hurts to see this, but we survived and that makes it better!

August 29, 2005. This is what Hurricane Katrina's winds of destruction did to the side of the building we were in during the storm. Two of these rooftops were torn off and landed on top of our apartment two doors over! It made the walls "breathe."

Ron Leblanc! My "Big Daddy"! Standing in front of his machine, a two-hundred-ton rig. This job was to reinforce the flood walls to the city of New Orleans. Ron is a crane operator for the largest construction company in Louisiana, Boh Bros. Construction Co. LLC.

Catherine enjoying a day of good weather.
(*Photo courtesy of Mr. Albert Cordell Thomas*)

At Essence Festival in New Orleans.
Met actor from Tyler Perry's *House of Payne*.
My husband, Ron Leblanc, took the picture.

Phyllis and Spike at afterparty at Sweet Lorraine's Jazz Club.
We just returned from a commercial for the New Orleans
Saints football team that featured Spike and a few others
from *When the Levees Broke*.

Getting a ride to the doctor is not so easy. I am not used to driving on the interstate, but I figure it won't be a problem. I go for a dentist appointment so I can finally get my gums and teeth healthy again. It has been a while since I've been to the dentist, since before Katrina. So I get my confidence up, and get on the highway. I'm nervous and stressed but I'm doing it. Listening to my cousin, Ricky Santiago, I put on some Rebirth Brass Band, and that does help calm me down some. I get in the dentist's office, and she's very nice. I immediately get a good vibe as soon as I walk in. She takes my blood pressure, and I'm like, "Wow, she's good." She tells me it's a little high, but that it's probably due to the drive over, and it being my first time doing the interstate. She waits another half hour, and it's higher. She and I get a little concerned. She waits another half hour, and it's higher still. Okay, now I'm starting to freak out, which is not a good thing, because this only makes it worse. I finish up my visit, and she suggests that I see my family doctor right away, but I suggest that I go to the emergency room. She agrees.

I call Ron and let him know what's going on and to meet me back at the trailer and take me to the emergency room. We get there, and when they take my blood pressure again it is even higher! Right away, I think that I'm about to die. I'm telling Ron what I'm feeling, and he's trying to tell me to calm down. They call me to go into the examination room. Next thing I know, I'm undressed, in a hospital gown, lying in a bed under blankets, in the hospital. I'm like, how in the fuck did I go from a dentist appointment to being in the emergency room? This is crazy! The nurse comes back in the room and takes my blood pressure again, and it's getting even higher. Oh, hell no. What the hell is going on? She takes my blood and leaves the room, but she leaves the blood pressure monitor cuff on my arm. In the meantime, I'm trying to turn around to look and see what it's saying. Ron is still telling me to relax. So I'm thinking it must be getting higher, and he doesn't want me to get upset, so that's why he keeps telling me to relax. How in the hell can I relax when my pressure is steadily going up? How? I swear I want to punch him dead in his face. I'm lying there thinking, okay, this is taking too long. Threatening to get up so I can see what's taking the nurse so long to come back. Ron walks to the door like he's actually doing something. Faking. I know he is faking, but good for him, because the nurse is walking back in the door. She says she wants me to go for X-rays. Oh shit, this must be serious. I continue questioning the nurse, and she's being pretty good about telling me there's nothing to worry about. Funny how people will say that shit to you when it's not them in the situation. You know what I mean?

So I go for the X-rays, and the technician is kind of a cute little youngster, and this makes it a little easier. Starting a conversation with someone is very easy for me, and so I do. He's a college student, and is planning to go out that evening with some friends and so on. He carries the conversation, realizing that I'm nervous, and that is pretty cool. We finish up and he says, "Looks pretty good. You're going to be all right." He wheels me back to the room, and they hook me back up to the blood pressure monitor, and my blood pressure starts to go down. And Ron tells me I shouldn't flirt. Whatever! It's a distraction of sorts, and it helps me to relax, and in the end my blood pressure returns to normal. Now

I'm lying there in this hospital bed, laughing at how in the hell I got here. That just goes to show you why I believe in Divine Intervention.

Had I not gone to the dentist and had she not taken my blood pressure, who knows what would have happened. The emergency room prescribes medicine to treat the blood pressure. Ron immediately goes to Walgreen's and buys me a blood pressure monitor. I've since gone to my regular doctor, and although my blood pressure read normal, she prescribed medicine for twelve months. After she examined me, she asked about a knot under my left arm. I told her that pre-Katrina I'd had a mammogram and that it was nothing but an ingrown hair that had caused it, but she was concerned and referred me to have another one done. We had no records to compare with, since the hospital that had done the test previously was destroyed by Hurricane Katrina (and from the looks of it, they will not be reopening any time soon).

So I go to the next examination for another mammogram, and the girl tells me that something doesn't look right according to the doctor, that I would need to have more X-rays done, and to go into the waiting room and she will call me right back. Okay, I'm sitting there, and I'm hearing these two women talk about their diagnosis and treatments and my heart begins to get full, and tears are in my eyes, but they will not fall. I jump up to get my cell phone and call Ron. I explain to him that, although it's probably nothing to worry about, I'm still upset. I go back and wait for her to call my name. She does more X-rays and again I have to go and wait for the doctor to say what's going on. She calls me back and tells me there is some type of "malignant calcification."

I ask her to explain and she does, but not completely, and then she crosses her fingers and tells me that the doctor says he'll see me back again in six months. Oh, but no. You can't tell a person that and then tell them to come back in six months—especially not a person like me and with the things that I've gone through in the past year and continue to go through. Another nurse comes out and I question her about my X-rays. She tells me it's nothing to worry about and come back in six months. Oh, the tears fall this time.

While I'm getting my clothes out of the safety locker, these two women come up to me and one asks if I'm the lady from the Spike Lee documentary. And once again, Divine Intervention, my worry is subsiding. I tell them yes I am, and they begin telling me how much I made the documentary easier to watch because of my humorous way of talking and telling my story. I immediately begin to tell them about my examination. All the time we're talking I see her cell phone in her hand, and I'm wondering why she's holding it like that. Is she recording our conversation? She notices my staring, and explains that she's been trying to call her husband since she first noticed me and he isn't answering. She says, "He's never going to believe who I'm talking to—he is crazy about you." I say, tell him, "What's up," and we finish our conversation. No sooner than I walk away from them do I go back to my worry about the examination.

When I get home to the trailer, Ron is sitting on the sofa. I fake confidence. I would rather suffer alone and not worry other people. So I explain to him that my regular doctor will be contacted, and everything's going to be okay. We go to bed and I cry all night. I'm wondering, who's going to raise my puppy and who's going to cook and take good care of Ron? I mean, how many women out there would know that he likes to eat a hot meal as soon as he gets in from work? How would they know that he doesn't like to argue? And that he has the heart of a peaceful and loving man? This was too much. I was delivered from the hurricane and the levees breaking and now this! What about my family? What about all of the people I'm supposed to help? What about my purpose in life? I pray and I eventually fall asleep.

I wake up the next morning, and I begin praying and crying, and when I tire of that my daily routine takes its place. My puppy, Brooklyn, is truly heaven sent. He's a little tiny Yorkshire terrier and gives so much unconditional love that it's impossible not to love him back. Now I understand why so many people refused to leave their pets during the storm. So I get past the "storm" of my doctor's visit, and call my regular doctor to make an appointment. She's not in that day and I'm like, maybe this is a bad sign. Okay, Phyllis, wake up, I say. This is exactly what the devil wants you to do, fall into self-pity and give up. I go to fix my bed, and Brooklyn jumps on it. I have to chase him. I can't catch him because he's dodging and running and playing. Finally, when I realize he could do this all day, I just lie across the bed laughing. He doesn't stop. He jumps at me as if he wants me to chase him and I laugh some more. Everyone should get a puppy.

From here on my day goes by quickly and with less thought of dying. I don't have any bad dreams that night. I get up the next morning, fix my pot of coffee and watch the microwave clock until it's 8:00 AM, and call the doctor's office to make an appointment. The receptionist says that the only dates they have available are two weeks from that day. I explain to her that this is not a good idea. I'm upset, and I need to see the doctor right away. She puts me on hold and asks my name again, and of course I say my full name: Phyllis Montana-Leblanc. The day I call is a Friday. She gives me the next day available, which is Monday. I'm feeling better already, and the weekend is a breeze. Ron comes with me, and I explain to the doctor about my mammogram visit and results. She looks at my X-rays and paperwork and explains my situation in more detail. I feel comfortable with her words, but I still want to see someone in that field. She asks if I'm taking the anxiety medicine she prescribed for me and I tell her, "No." She then gives me a prescription for Xanax, which is specifically for my fear of thunderstorms.

Okay, Ron and I get on our way and go to the pharmacist, who is making serious bank off of us, and I'm guessing, the entire city of New Orleans since Katrina. I get the prescription filled, and we are on our way home. I still don't feel safe until I see this breast specialist. So I get through the days until my appointment with the specialist. She's very nice from the jump. And she keeps looking at me, and then asks if I have been a patient of hers. I say, "No, this is my first time visiting with you." And she goes about explaining things to me. She is very nice, pleasant, and professional, but most of all, she is knowledgeable. That is the best part.

Then she looks at me again and asks where she has seen my face before. I tell her, "Maybe it's from the documentary, *When the Levees Broke.*" She smiles and says, "Yes, that's where

I know you from." I do that a lot. When somebody recognizes me from the documentary, they try to remember where they've seen my face. It's fun seeing them trying to remember. Sometimes I tell them that maybe we went to school together or we used to work together. They get a kick out of it and so do I. The one thing that is guaranteed from this is that it always gets them to smile. One of my jobs in life is to make people smile or laugh. It just seems to me that we should have more laughter and less crying. I tell my family, Spike, and others that I don't get what people see in me, but if it makes them smile and be glad to see me, hey, what the hell? It's all Gumbo, Red Beans, and Rice to me, you know? Like I said before, I got—like so many others—screwed twice, once by Hurricane Katrina and then a lifetime by the corps of engineers and the levee board.

Through all of life's trials and tribulations, God has been with me, and just like Psalm 23 says, He didn't say you weren't going to go through it, He said He would be there with you. And I love that. Sure, we cry, and we moan and groan when life is giving us the tough, rough, and seemingly unbearable, but do we not go on? I know I have. We can play the blame game for the rest of our lives, but the real deal about the Katrina tragedy in New Orleans is to make sure that it doesn't happen again.

I don't have a degree in psychology, but I have learned lessons from life, so that gives me a life-experience degree. That's what I'm sticking with. One of the most hurtful things in life is to have trusted someone, only to have them turn on you and bite you in the ass. Now that's some shit that will make you "go there." Five minutes of thoughtless anger can change you in ways that last a lifetime. I know that there will always be some people who won't agree with what I say, or will be offended that I use cuss words in the same voice that I use to give Glory to God. But nobody, and I mean nobody, knows my relationship with God.

My contribution to this world is not through the movies like Spike Lee or television like Oprah Winfrey. My contribution is within the space of my walking, driving, and everyday communication and contact with people. I have had people come up to me with negative comments about drug use in my past and I will talk with them about it, or anybody else, and you know why? Because I don't do them anymore. Because of sexual and physical abuse in my young childhood I developed low self-esteem. I inflicted pain on myself. But some things are between God and me. I no longer visit my past unless it benefits me to remind me of what not to do, or to read a person that I'm dealing with. All I want to do in life is to help people get past the things that hurt them, and move to the happiness of life and the joy of God's Love. I believe that we should never forget the wrongs in life because they remind us of who people really are and what they will and can do to us.

Playing the "if only" tapes in our mind isn't really helpful. If only Mayor C. Ray Nagin had gotten us help before the four days. If only Governor Kathleen Blanco had gotten us help before the four days. If only President George W. Bush had gotten us help before the four days. What really matters is that they didn't. I think the true judgment is when God puts in front of them what they were really doing while people old and young and even babies were drowning.

That's why I am satisfied with what God has given to me, and that's looking in the mirror at my own face and eyes to make sure that I don't repeat wrongs that I have myself done.

We take on public positions and then we don't want that same public to judge us, but it is what comes with the territory. Even with this story, my story, some people are going to like it and some people are not. What matters to me most is if I help someone with my words of encouragement, or if I cause someone to laugh or smile. I am sorry for all those who lost someone special and dear to them. I wish I could have been there to help, but I was in my own hurt and I was lost in my own mind. My life is now and forever changed.

Ever since God delivered me from the bondages of other people, it's been *on*. If you like me then that's fine, we can talk. If you don't, then don't be around me or in my face. Simple as that. Nobody in the free world has to like anybody. Thinking otherwise is something I never understood and probably never will. Before and after Katrina I have dealt with phony-ass people who smile in my face and mean me no good: blood even more than strangers. I had a relative call my sister Lisa, who lives in Brooklyn, and tell her that I was "acting ghetto." Yes, on the documentary. One of my aunts called Lisa and said that she thought I was "ghetto" and then asked my sister what she thought about it. Of course, my sister, my baby sister, said she liked how I spoke because she is also "real" and tells it like it is, okay? Now this same person has committed all kinds of ghetto acts then and now. This is why when folks say shit about you, just look at that person's life and then it won't matter at all. I have never claimed to be a saint and nor do I now. To be perfectly honest with you, I don't see sainthood in my future, as far as the qualifications go. Now, what God deems to be worthy is another story.

 So why do we waste this wonderful life that God gave us hating each other and discriminating against each other for choices in life? From what I have read in the Bible, we all are dirty cloths and fall short of the Glory of God. So, who in the hell made those of us the final judge? We, that's who. Our selfish-ass selves. Now, our opinions, our comments about wrongdoing, I'm good with it. We are humans, and we express ourselves, but the hate thing, it's worse than the worst disease.

The murder rate in New Orleans is back in stride again. On our ninth murder in the city, a woman and her husband were shot. The woman died and the husband, with their baby in his arms, was shot several times but survived, and so did the baby. As I sat and watched this on the local news,

I cried. How could someone do this? I also cried the previous weeks when Dinneral Shavers was murdered; he was a member of the Hot 8 Brass Band, a local group here in the city. The couple and their child were white, Mr. Shavers was black. There was a march on city hall after the woman's murder. All of these people, black and white, all races were out at city hall demanding that the police department and the city stop these crimes. The lady's murder was number nine in the city, and Dinneral's was number eight. My confusion was, where was the march for murders number one, two, three, four, five, six, seven, and eight? Why are we in an "epidemic state" when no one else but blacks are being murdered? I am confused about this and wonder if anyone has an answer to this.

We seem satisfied with just calling it black-on-black crime until it happens in a nonblack neighborhood. It is horrible when anyone loses a loved one to crime. Why are blacks not out marching for an end to crime? I know there have been some pastors and the like out now and again, but none that I can remember marching on city hall. I don't know how to stop crime. Until we stop acting according to the color of our skin color we are forever stuck. This was just something that came to my mind and I hope for an answer. My heart goes out to all of the families that have lost everything that they owned and then have to deal with the loss of a loved one to crime. I can't say much more than that right now.

I can't save the world all at once, but I believe that I can save one person at a time, and it doesn't matter what the class, race, or choice in life. It all has to come down to love. Where there's love there is understanding. Where there's understanding there's communication. Where there's communication, there's resolution. Where there's resolution, there's peace and harmony within the human race and not just tolerance of one another. If we could have more of one person being kind and generous to another, not based on how much money they have or what shade of color their skin is or how they speak or what school they went to or how or if they went to school—damn, I know I'm asking for a lot but it is not too much. I'm just being *Phyllisophical* and nobody has to agree with me. I am but one person and sometimes one person can make a difference. I just pray that God blesses me with the wisdom, knowledge, and grace to share it with the world.

If we can't take care of each other how will humanity survive and what is God going to say to us when we meet Him? We all fight over which religion is best and whose is the worst. We all call Him a different name and pull apart the Bible and some make it what they want it to be to serve themselves rather than serving others. I believe in everything in the Bible. That's me. You believe what you want and don't try shoving it down my throat and we can talk. Again, look at the person who's telling it to you. You can look at me the same way (oh, like I have to tell you that one) because, like I said, I never claimed to be a saint, Christian, or anyone in a position to guide. I just do what I do and I am about love and togetherness, but I will tell you this: I will not have anyone hurting me and allow it to happen. I've been down that path and it's not good for me.

This story is about what I went through during Hurricane Katrina and its aftermath. Hurricane Katrina brought to the surface a lot of things, good and bad. I have been offered the privilege of sharing my story. Remember, this is my story, how I felt, and what I want to share. This is not a black story, an angry story, or a judgment story. I'm just an average woman who is happy with herself and joyful in the Lord God Almighty. I am not cured of my fears of thunderstorms just yet, but the love from people of New Orleans and all over the country I have spoken to has helped me begin and continue my healing. I thank each and every one of you.

A lot of times we don't know just how much we help someone just by smiling or stopping to have a word with them. Sometimes we save a life and we don't even know it. I believe that everything is by design. Everything that we are going through has already been written. My cussing will cease to exist one day and I will be so glad, because I am tired of it. Just like I got tired of all the shit I used to do back in the day—I became tired of it and I stopped. I hope that you all like what I have had to say, but if you don't, at least use it for "food for thought." I could use the saying, "if I've helped one person then my job is complete," but that would be bullshit, because I want to help a whole lot of people. Just because I'm black don't mean you can't see me. Just because I'm positive don't mean a negative can't approach me. Just because I didn't ask for it but you knew I needed it didn't mean you had to deny me of it.

Sometimes we are complacent and comfortable with a relationship and we take it for granted. It doesn't matter what type of relationship it is, whether it is friendship, marriage, or just a companion. A true friend is there when you need them and one should not have to beg for help when they already know what is needed. This is not for any one person, it is for all who read this. If you take it personally, then you must be who I'm talking about. Always remember to look at the rating of a movie, and you will not be surprised by its contents. Always look up a word in the dictionary if you don't know or aren't sure of its meaning. And if that guy in the corner store asks me one more time if Spike Lee paid me, while he's standing there buying E-Z Wider papers, I'm going to have to let him have it. After about three or four people asked me this question, I'm not going to lie—I started getting a little pissed off. So I said what I'll do is, when someone asks me if Spike Lee is pay-ing me and what the amount is, I will ask them for their social security number, and when they say that information is private, then I'll just point my finger at them. Now, if that doesn't work, well I don't know, maybe we can just put it out there, that it will never be anyone's business what someone's money is, and especially a stranger. I mean, come on now, I know some young ladies from New Orleans who would straight cuss your ass out if you ask them something like that. It was funny though.

Like I said before, we have to get some good out of this devastation. Like my sister Catherine, who lost her hus-band to liver cancer in 2004, and this is where Ron and me have our trailer, on their property. Since Michael's death she has not been able to dream about him and on the morning when he would have turned forty-three years old, she awoke to the memory of a beautiful dream. She said she was walk-ing in a beautiful garden with somebody, and she couldn't see their face but she was having a full conversation. There were ducks and she could hear water but couldn't see it. There were sunflowers and hummingbirds. Then the person said to her: "Have you ever wondered to take a look?" And she said, "Or to hear the sound of a babbling brook." Then the voice said, "Sometimes you have to take a small stick and tap the flowers to see the hummingbirds, red cardinals, and other birds." Then she did it; she took a small stick and tapped the flowers, and the birds started to fly out of the flowers. Then she woke up. She got up and went into the kitchen to get breakfast ready for her son Nicholas and there are these pictures that she uses to help him learn and all but one was up on the wall. She looked on the floor and one picture was on the floor and it was the picture of their son, with his backpack. She placed her hand over her heart and let out a deep gasp, and threw her head back and laughed as she spoke the words, "Thank you, God, thank you, Michael." This was the spirit of God giving her the peace that she'd been searching for and on this day. On his date of earthly birth, love was ever flowing as the love that sustains us through times of loss.

So in essence, we never lose a loved one, we gain an eternity of love. A love that never ends but only carries us through the life that we live. And this is where they say, "When God does something, sometimes he does it in a big way and all at once." What more could she ask for? I miss my Catherine and my mother and my nephew, Nicholas, being here where we call "home." I notice that as much as I cry some days and others I just lie in bed, I am blessed to wake up each of these days and keep moving forward. I have

learned that life will be filled with tests, trials, and tribulations, but as long as I've got King Jesus, it will be okay.

You see, one person can make a difference, but one person can't fight all of the battles. There are battles that we
sometimes must leave to another. These chosen ones may not
do it in the absolute way that we think they should, but the
battle is being fought. Not in a million years would I want to
be the president of the United States. I would not want to be
the governor or mayor—well, maybe one of these two, but it
is a lot that they have to shoulder. At the same time, if you
run for one of these offices, aren't you aware of what you will
have to deal with?

I've spoken with several different people about writing
this memoir and when I tell them that it may top out at one
hundred pages, they usually ask, "Is that all?" My answer to
that is, "I have many, many more stories to tell, and a great
deal of them are horrific." I can always write a continuance
to this because this story tells itself and it can go on for
a very long time. A lot of people tell me to let Spike Lee
know that there's more to be told about Hurricane Katrina
and the levees breaking and I do, but there is a process to
this just like there is a process to life. I have since forgiven
those who left us to rot and die all of those days. I have to
if I want to move forward, but I tell you, every time they
say something, it will always be doubt first, then maybe,
then let's see, then, naw, still don't trust them. It's like a
young cousin of mine, Kerry Santiago, says: "Go head with
dat, stop playing." This was some "real shit" and if it didn't
wake up some folks, then more power to them. That's all I
have to say on that one.

We were given something during Hurricane Katrina that a great many people have yet to see and that is the response to a devastating natural disaster. We all wonder how the government can spend billions, even trillions on war, and here a bill for an increase for minimum wages can't get passed and if it does it will be spread out over some years. Come on now. It's time, people, it's time to show an act of kindness to someone you do not even know. It's time to pay it forward, share the wealth, make lemonade when life gives you lemons, all that shit. Each of us has to do something in this life that is for the good. We already know what the bad is, so why not try the good? Tears come to my eyes as I'm writing this, because I have always had the spirit to change things. Especially from bad to good or bad to better, however you want to put it, but as long as you understand. As a young child I heard the Sam Cooke song "A Change Is Gonna Come," and always felt pain in my heart, but never understood why. Then when I became a young woman I decided to ask my mom about the song, and she told me that this was the song that was playing when her and my dad broke up. Does anybody else see this connection and the "design" of it all? This was already written for my hurt and pain of the past to finally get put in its place.

Hurricane Katrina was devastating but how much of nature's beauty can also bring death? Think about it. Now the levees breaking, that's another story. Those levees were not supposed to break, had the corps of engineers and the levee board did what they were supposed to do. They know what they did and didn't do and for me, just for me, that's between them, God, and brothers like Spike Lee. The people who come up to me now hardly ask about Spike Lee; they ask about me and tell me how proud they are of me and how good a job I did in helping them to show the painful sights in the documentary. I didn't do it to make people laugh. There was no script. Spike didn't tell me what to say and had no idea of what I was going to say, but he knew that only the true Phyllis Montana-Leblanc would tell it like it is. And I did. When people ask me how does it feel to be a star, all I tell them is I don't know because I'm just trying to get to Heaven. Each day is a battle and a Spiritual Battle at that (those are harder, because that old devil never sleeps) but I do it, with God's Blessing and Mercy, I do it.

In my old thinking I always knew that there was something good in this life that would come to me, and it did, the only thing is that it was always there and I just needed to have the courage to survive the bad. We all have it in us but we just have to have the faith and courage to look for it and not get tired so quickly and give up so quickly. If you are a young girl and your boyfriend deals drugs and you want a better life, tell him and don't be afraid of letting go to get to the better in life that God has planned for you. I'll drop in some of my poetry that I've written since Hurricane Katrina and hope that you all enjoy it, and it gives you something to think about. Pain is pain, no matter how you get it or who gives it to you, and you are the only one who can put it in its place and move forward. I don't know anyone who wants to be in pain, so if it helps to talk to someone then do it. Sometimes talking to someone who knows nothing about you can help.

Then there are those people who think that I was such a fool for talking so real about my experience and I should not have done it. I'm not going to tell you what they can kiss. I really am trying to stop the cussing and I am intelligent enough to know that it won't happen overnight, but I am not one to give up. I suggest that you do the same. Don't Give Up. Life will never ask you if you need more time to get back on your feet. It will keep on going and that is a natural, real fact. Don't do something that you don't want to do. I remember somebody asking me if it was true that Spike Lee was using me and what's the word they used? Exploited. My answer was surprisingly without cuss words. Hmmm. Must have caught me on one of those days when as soon as I woke up I started praying and surrounding myself with the Full Armor of God, because all I said was, "No, he did not. All that he has quoted me in any magazine as saying, is that I told it to him and those were my actual words." Done. No matter what you do in life there will always be some people you cannot or won't please, but that's life and you just can't let it get you down. You have to be strong and you have to hold on.

There are still not many public schools open for children to attend. This is so freaking crazy because it's like someone doesn't want black children to be educated. The reason I am able to say this is because if you look at all of the areas in the city of New Orleans, we are the only ones that have this problem. My nephew Nicholas can't even come back because there is no public education for children with autism. So the only time I can see his face is from memory, and pictures that Catherine mails to me once a year, or during our visit to Texas during Christmas. I feel like this is a time of slavery. This is from an African-American point of view. Families were torn apart. Mothers couldn't find their children because they were taken from them and sent to different states without them. I didn't know where my own mother, sister, and nephew were for at least a week. That's because the people in charge of the helicopters separated us and then lied, telling us that we would be on the next helicopter after them. Our world changed from being working-class citizens with hopes and dreams for our future to being homeless, hungry, and unwanted. This happened in the United States of America!

Oh sure, I still keep going. I even still smile and make people laugh and smile every chance that I get. This does not change the fact that my memory of what was done to us by all of the people in charge of our city, state, and country will never be erased. I am speaking for people of my race because the people left behind were predominately African-American, but this is also an entirety of people who were abandoned while idiots decided what was legal and what was not legal. All of this while people were drowning, even in their own homes. Then after the long time that it took to drain the water from the city, dogs began chewing and eating the bodies of people who lay dead in the streets. This was happening to people in New Orleans, Louisiana! I am not crazy, but this shit nearly pushed me over the cliff and I am not bullshitting you. The disbelief that something like this could happen in our country still has not emptied out of my mind.

I refuse to give up and I refuse to die. This is not the way it is supposed to be, but that doesn't mean that some people care about that or us. I said it once and I'll say it again: yes,

I spoke about thoughts of suicide. I was tired and did not want to face the reality of my government showing me to my face and to the world that we did not mean shit to them. And they are still showing us that we don't mean shit to them, by making it close to impossible for people to move back home. I still can't believe that the mother of the president of the United States of America has not apologized for her statements. How in the hell did she know who was poor and who wasn't? And that since they were already from poverty, sleeping on a fucking cot in the Astrodome was better than where they came from? What kind of shit is that? The apple and the tree, the apple and the tree!

We are told to forget about slavery, but down here in Louisiana, slave plantations are still up and running and being preserved for history, white history. Yet it's not okay for us to remember the raping, beating, and human bondage of African-Americans. Do you know that some black people actually have their wedding receptions in places like that? I know everyone is entitled to his or her choices in life, but come on now! This is a fact for everyone, everywhere: I would have been a slave for a total of twenty-four hours. I'll leave the rest to your imagination and what you have seen of me in the documentary. One day we all will realize that we are all being fucked by the same prick and dick of divide and conquer. The only difference is that it's on different levels. It's kind of like a black and a white going into a store and all eyes are on the black and the white is doing all of the stealing. Racism is alive and kicking and I don't see it ever going away. My best foot forward is to treat people the way they treat me. I will get back up again. That is guaranteed, God willing. I will not be weak forever from what I went through during Hurricane Katrina. There are so many untold stories of horror that need to be told to the world. I still have nightmares about drowning and starving to death while dogs attack me, eating at my body. Sometimes in my dreams I see the mayor of New Orleans, the governor of Louisiana, and the president of the United States watching me die and they are laughing and they are all saying that I'm just one less nigger in the world. Then there are many nights when I don't dream at all. I'm starting to take pleasure in the things that I used to love, like watching butterflies or sunsets, and it feels like normal times. Then I turn around and I see the trailer that Ron and I still live in. Nobody is doing anything about the apartments' price gouging. A lot of people may have been poor but they were able to afford their poverty. They paid their bills and worked and they are survivors. A lot of rich people are buying up the land down here in New Orleans because they know that this will make them more money. A great many volunteers have been here in the city and I still see them here gutting out homes and helping to rebuild. I am very grateful to them.

I was standing on the porch of the trailer a few days ago and a woman recognized me from the documentary and we started a conversation. We ended up talking about how in the area where we live, they don't have any more shopping centers for us because the city tore them down. All we have right now is corner stores and a few businesses. She told me a story of when her brother and some other people were walking in the water after the storm and they saw an alligator with a body in its mouth. A woman who was with them has said that after seeing that, she will never set foot in New Orleans again.

To say that Hurricane Katrina traumatized me would be a flat-out lie. I was traumatized by being left behind for so long without my family. We were left to die. I will never forget this and nobody in this country should have to go through this. Greed. Greed for money is ruining this world. And until we realize that not one of us can have it all, we will continue to be sacrificial lambs. And race really doesn't matter when someone wants to have it all to him- or herself. We all need to stand for something positive or else we are going to fall for the negative and it comes in many shapes, fashions, and faces. I may not be where I want to or need to be in my life right now, but I thank God that I'm not where I used to be.

It's time to start healing us and taking matters and our lives into our own hands. We have been shown to our faces what we can trust and depend on. We must not focus on what divides us but rather on what brings us together. Stop judging someone because of their skin color, or how they dress, or how much money they have. Shit, I'm broke and in my opinion you couldn't ask for a better friend. Well, not broke, but financially challenged would be a better word. I have learned over many years that not all white people are evil, just like not all black people are lazy. So in essence, not just the levees broke: a whole lot more broke along with those levees and it's time we as human beings start putting this world back together the right way. We all know how bad we can make this world; I now challenge everyone to see how good we can make this world.

I am still healing from August 29, 2005, and my prayers

are for all of those in the city of New Orleans and the Gulf Coast states. Hurricane Katrina exposed so many things in myself and in this world. She exposed that racism is still strong and prominent. She exposed in me that being weak does not mean defeat. She exposed that not all white people hate black people. I am standing on my own two feet and today is the first day of the rest of my life. Cussing and anger do not define who Phyllis Montana-Leblanc is completely. They are the weak side of me. There is more to me than meets the eye and the world is about to see just how much I care for all people, no matter what their skin color, class, or level of education. Hurricane Katrina hurt me but she also inspired me to heal not only myself but others as well. People across the world should each adopt a family in need down here in New Orleans and become a part of history in helping to rebuild lives and not just the things that have no beating heart.

"See you in the Gumbo, just don't be the shrimp."

# PHYLLISOPHICAL
# FOOD FOR THOUGHT

Hurricane Katrina, with winds blowing out electric power, pushing twenty-foot waves of water and winds before her and behind her, she walked as a woman scorned. It was as if she was in memory of all the wrong that had been done to her, and as the bile rose up from the bowels of hell that was inside her, feeling the acidic burn in the back of her throat, she began to vomit from all that would cleanse, in search for a new beginning, a beginning of destruction, rebuild, then start over the right way. Hurricane Katrina was the Bob Marley song "Redemption" in the city of New Orleans, Louisiana, on August 29, 2005. As a result of the corps of engineers' neglect to repair and maintain correctly the levees that are supposed to protect the citizens, the city was flooded by Hurricane Katrina's power, and this too happened on August 29, 2005. The Gulf Coast states were obliterated along with us and left to fend for themselves as well.

The streets where I walked and played as a young child

had swollen bodies floating on them. This was my home and it will never be the same, so I wonder now, "Where is the place that I once called home?" Imagine where you now live whether you've been there one year or forty-four years and a storm blows through and you survive it, but the walls around your city come crashing down and five, ten, fifteen or twenty feet of water come bursting into your home, and you have to run to your attic with a hammer, beat a hole in the roof, and climb through it.

Then you sit on this rooftop and wait in the dark for a helicopter or boat to come and rescue you. Four days pass by and nobody comes. You have been left to die and you begin to have these feelings of giving up and wondering where is the God you believed in and prayed to for help. You give up and slowly put one foot in the black water with dead bodies floating past you and then you put another foot in and slowly descend into the grave that was not supposed to be yours. You hold your breath as long as you can, and water begins to fill your lungs, and the fear that is all-consuming has you hearing the beat of drums, when you realize that it's your heart you are hearing so loudly, so deafening that you can literally hear it, and it becomes too much and the only solution is to drink in the black water to stop the pain and fear so you can rest and sleep eternally and the last thing you see is the bodies of your neighbors and their children floating by, with the flies and maggots eating their flesh.

The waters have gone away, and the trees and flowers have grown back again in the city of New Orleans, but the smell of neglect, torture, abandonment, and death still flows through like those black waters. It has been three years and the smell is still here. I could ask why did this happen to us for the rest of my life and I will never believe the many, many answers that I give myself or get from others. I could blame this city's mayor, this state's governor, or the president of our United States, but that will not help me sleep the same ever again. What I have done is seen what man can and will do to you without even blinking an eye. Trusting in a Higher Being is what is saving my sanity and understanding of what happened to us on August 29, 2005. I call Him God. I call Him Jesus Christ, My Lord and Savior! This is my belief and that's that. I want the people, the person who reads this story, this memoir, to embrace it. Can you imagine what you saw on television as being your life when the media was covering Hurricane Katrina? Our government is considered to be the most powerful in this world, as we know it. Our leaders who we voted into office and pay our tax dollars to, turned their heads while citizens were drowning, committing suicide, being on the brink of starvation, here, in the United States of America!!!! Movie director and filmmaker Spike Lee chose to come to our city and show the world proof of the heads who were turned away. He made the documentary, *When the Levees Broke.* It is beyond words what was shown in the documentary and there is definitely more than what was seen. As Spike said, "It's not over with this documentary, this story is still not finished."

At this writing it has been two years and four months and in the area where I still live in a FEMA trailer, there is no hospital or clinic. Only a few schools have reopened, but our "area" leaders are more concerned about a shopping mall and high-priced apartment complexes and homes.

What I see is "Man's inhumanity to man." Homes are more important to human beings surviving and living. People here are still fighting to get money to rebuild their homes from a program ironically called "Road Home." There are working homeless camping out in tents in front of city hall because of price gouging. The apartments where they lived pre-Katrina are no longer affordable. And on the local news we see that the city of New Orleans is now evicting these homeless people. I mean, how in the hell do you evict homeless people from the street? These people are not homeless by choice, you know? Some people are saying that we should be back on our feet by now and for us to stop holding FEMA or the government responsible for our lives. They are right in a sense, yes, we should not depend on those who failed us on August 29, 2005. Look at what they've done so far. But, see, here's the catch; they still have not cleaned up the mess they caused in the first place. Clean up your damn mess and be done with it, and we can go on with our lives. I have overcome and dealt with many, many "storms" in my life before the levees broke and drowned my city, my home, but I have never taken such a beating to my mind and heart such as what was done to us during the season of Hurricane Katrina. First I was diagnosed with high blood pressure, then I was taken off (at my request) those medications, and placed on treatment for post-traumatic stress disorder. Then, just a few days ago, I was diagnosed with rheumatoid arthritis. I was thinking that it was due to typing or lifting and moving boxes with our belongings but it was becoming more and more painful and waking me at night. You know what it was from in my opinion? In a FEMA trailer, there is a bed, or rather a mattress, that lies on top of a thin board. Under this piece of board is a storage area you can access by either raising the board or going outside of the trailer and opening a small door. So all of the cold air that is outside during the winter months is under this "bed" that we—my husband and I—have slept on for over a year. I mean, you could actually feel the cold air blowing on the sides of the bed and the "headboard" where our pillows were. So I came up with an idea to stop it and stuffed bed sheets and bath towels around the perimeter of the "mattress." But because we've been here so long the cold has gotten into my bones and joints in my knees, back, neck, feet, and hands. When I think of all that we have gone through and are going through I am not complaining. No, this is not complaining, this is testimony of the Spirit that lives in me, the Spirit of God. My thoughts continue to return to "man's inhumanity to man." The city of New Orleans is now demolishing four low-income housing projects and in their place is building new mixed-income housing. This means that people who lived there before Hurricane Katrina will have no affordable place to live. This means that they have to wait until something is built before they can move in. Again, "man's inhumanity to man."

It seems to me that the survival of human life here in our city is similar to political debates, where two opposing sides try and determine who will win the war of words, when what should be priority are lives. I look at some rich people who purchase things they want and the cost is phenomenal, and I wonder how many people that money could help find somewhere to lay their head and have a home. I also look at the other side of the coin, where some people don't try hard enough to bring themselves up. How can I expect someone to help the "poor," when the "poor" has just come from the beauty salon with nails and hair done up nice, and she complains that she can't get any money from FEMA? How do I defend some people who go clubbing every weekend, with no job, and return to a FEMA trailer as if it's home? How do I defend that? I defend that behavior by saying that our way of thinking has to change. We as an African-American race or black race are looked down upon because others see a great many of us as not being self-reliant. We as a race of people are so strong, beautiful, and intelligent, that it breaks my heart not seeing us reach our full potential.

Now, I include my own self in that number. I chose to let life's trials and tribulations get and keep me down for many, many years but I have always refused to give up. Yes, I thought about giving up, but something inside of me knew that God has a greater plan for me. Greater is He who is in me than he who lives in the world. If you survived Hurricane Katrina and the levees breaking, don't you think or would like to think that you were allowed to be here for a reason? I believe that reason is not to continue in your old ways but to follow new ways, better ways for your life and purpose here on earth. Very few of us live to reach seventy-five years old let alone one hundred years old, so if your earthly time here is so short, why would you waste it doing things that don't make a difference? I want to be remembered not for the bad things I did and said but the purposeful and meaningful things that helped someone smile who was having a bad day, or speaking kind, understanding words to someone who was maybe contemplating ending their lives. Yes, I'm sure things will still piss me off from time to time and I will probably "go off" on the situation but I am daily meditating on my attitude toward the situation rather than the situation itself. You know what I mean? I love the fact that I was treated horribly by people in my past and all of my trials and tribulations with physical, sexual, emotional, and mental abuse, not because I enjoyed it, but because those situations made me who I am, the total opposite of what was done to me. I do the best I can to promote love, togetherness, peace, and all-around smiles and laughter. What you see of me is what you get of me and I love the feeling of love. I believe and have seen the human nature of forgetfulness. We've all sat and watched horrors on the daily news and we cry and mourn for those dead, dying, starving, or murdered, and suffering of all kinds. Then we forget about it until it comes up again in conversation or someone or something sparks our memory of it.

As I mentioned before, some people believe that we should forget about how we were treated during Hurricane Katrina and after, and that we should be back on our feet by now, like it's over. But it's not! We are still living in Hurricane Katrina's aftermath because the people responsible for our losses still have not owned up to it. You cannot fix what you don't acknowledge, and this is why people are still suffering in New Orleans to this day! The things that I personally experienced during and after Hurricane Katrina has affected and changed my life forever and has also moved my life forward. I will never again allow myself to wait on "man's" word to leave or not to leave, when a hurricane is predicted to make landfall. I will and have made it a point to put money on the side just in case we need to leave home. That is what some people don't understand about the way we in New Orleans feel about our city: it is our home and, yes, a great deal of us here have never traveled abroad, but does that mean that we should be forced to leave? I mentioned to my husband just the other day that I felt like I was becoming "less intelligent," like my intelligence was being depleted by living in a FEMA trailer for so long. He just looked at me, shook his head, and laughed. Saying, "Phyllis, you think too much." I'm so serious about this because when you live in a small space all you see is that small space. I can walk my dog, Brooklyn, three times a day, run daily errands and such, but that's it. FEMA says that the trailers are not safe to live in because of formaldehyde emanation, but I have always kept my air vents on and windows open, but how in the hell would I look complaining about the poisons with a cigarette in my hand? Stress will kill you quicker than formaldehyde—hell, I challenge anyone who does not believe what it's like to live how we have been forced to live since Hurricane Katrina and have a different attitude about it. It is nothing like you see on television, and the absolute, most real, and actual account of some of what we went through and what was done to us has been, to date, Spike Lee's HBO documentary, *When the Levees Broke*. I firmly believe if each and every one of us does his or her share of spreading love and not hate we could change this world. Yes, there are going to be those who spread and teach hate, but wouldn't it be just grand to conquer them? I mean to conquer hate with love! It could happen if each time someone showed hate or discrimination or judgment on any one of us we showed love in return. There is a difference between anger and hate, you know? Anger lasts but a moment or two, okay, sometimes for me three or four—okay, five! But hate, hate lasts a lifetime for some people. I mean just look back at the people who hated blacks and hung them from trees and burned their bodies, just because of the color of their skin. Then they teach these same things to their children and grandchildren, and it becomes a part of "continuing education." As a child I used to often wonder what it would be like to be white and treated nicely and with respect, and then I grew up. I used to be angry at how it took my mom longer to comb my hair than that of my four sisters. I used to cry sometimes because I thought I was ugly because my skin color was darker than almost all of my family members. You see, all of these things I had not thought about for years until Hurricane Katrina and how we were treated. All of those old feelings of hurt, pain, and despair broke open, and that's why I could not get the words "Not Just the Levees Broke" out of my mind, because it's true. When those levees broke, my whole world broke apart, and I still feel some of those feelings to this day.

Today, as I am writing this, I am still living with the residual effects of man's greed. Had those levees been fixed the way and when they were supposed to, this might not have happened. But we learn, don't we? Life is a constant lesson, each day that we awake there will be a lesson to learn. Those who don't see it that way are doomed to repeat the same mistakes and life will stay hard. I am so grateful that Spike Lee chose to come down to New Orleans and do the documentary about what we were feeling and how we were let down and left to die, because if I had not been able to express my feelings I probably would have just given up on life and died. I give all the Glory and Thanks to the Lord above and I believe that all the people who cared enough to help us in so many ways were sent by God, and Spike Lee is one of those people. The funny thing about Spike Lee is that he doesn't look for thanks or seem to go for all of the attention that in my opinion he truly deserves. He has a vision of something and he puts it out there. He's not this "angry" person that I see a lot of media portraying him as. He gets pissed off at injustice and loves the human race. He, like me, loves his black people and I don't see anything wrong with that. It's like some people want African-Americans to forget about slavery, because "it happened so long ago," but down here in New Orleans, Louisiana, slave plantations are still preserved! So why is it okay for some to preserve their history of human bondage and those whose ancestors were those in bondage shouldn't talk about it, or bring it up, or just plain forget about it? That's just crazy thinking. August 29, 2005, and the days, months, and years that followed were a wake-up call for me, and I hope for many, many, many others. It made me think about my purpose here on earth, how I treat people, how we can change the way we live and think, and, most of all, it helped me to see that there really are still people in this world who know and show love. Real love is when you do something straight from the heart for another and put yourself in that person's shoes. Whether you believe in the theory of Darwin and evolution, or Yahweh, or the Almighty God and the Son, Christ Jesus, do we not still see the human in each of us? I'm not perfect, and neither is anyone that I have ever met or believe will ever meet. So, how can we judge one another on something over which we have no control, such as skin color? Yes, Hurricane Katrina started it all, but the levees breaking opened up more than concrete walls that were supposed to protect us in New Orleans. That is why the title *Not Just the Levees Broke* is what I chose because when those levees broke they broke open a past I had long forgotten. A past of pain and suffering, loneliness and abandonment. They broke open mistrust, where I had just begun to trust again. They broke open hurtful people from my past life, and sent my mind back to fear and dread. So, when people look at the worst disaster in U.S. history, there is a deeper story here, and if you want to know more all you have to do is come down to New Orleans and talk to some of the people who still live here and they will tell you of the unjust way in which people are being treated. It's almost as if time has rolled back to the 1960s, and if you're black you're back to being considered a worthless "nigger." If you're "nonblack" you now see that we all got screwed or are getting screwed. Each day my Lord and Savior Jesus Christ awakes me, I am thankful and rejoice. Each day is a struggle, but with His mercy and grace, I am able to raise up and keep on keeping on. I pray that each and every one of us stops for a moment and thinks about changing hate to love, shaking someone's hand, smiling at someone in greeting, telling someone to have a nice day, or simply thanking someone for little things. I believe that we are all intelligent enough to know that change is possible. So, when you see my face and you look into my eyes, go beyond them and believe that when I look back at you I am showing to you my soul. The soul of a woman who survived. I am not a victim, I am a survivor! May you grow, love, and share the love that lives in each of us. Peace.

# KATRINA POEMS

## AND THIS TOO SHALL PASS

Today there was a storm and Phyllis didn't run
for cover,

Well, she did but stayed put and didn't run to the
"other."

There were no tears, no alcohol, or pills to calm
the fear,

She took what came and even listened to hear.

Sleep came peacefully and Ron left to make sure
"I'd handle the storm,"

Angry with him in the aftermath, for it is <u>my</u> choice
to make it the "norm."

Day by day I will have to get through this mess of
coming back to strong,

I have no choice if I want to continue living, being
right has to go against what is wrong.

This will pass. I know that it will. I have to get over
this fear of dying,

I have to keep going on, for my purpose of living. I
have to keep trying.

Scared, I still am, and I know that it will be hard to beat,

But how will I know what I am strong enough for if I already accept defeat?

I can scratch myself until I bleed for the reason of distraction,

Or I can bring it all together and simply change my reaction.

Y'all don't know what it did to me to come close to death by drowning,

This is how I survive sometimes, by taking the pain and saying, "I'm just clowning."

And this too shall pass. Is what I believe and what I keep saying.

And this too shall pass, is all I've got to just keep praying.

## ANOTHER STORM LAST NIGHT

I tried to sleep, as I heard the walls tumbling down
around me, the dark sky lit by the flashing light,

Breathing hard through my mouth, wondering if
God would show some mercy, some mercy, to calm
my fright.

In my mind I yelled, "Take it! Take it!" but it did
not hold. "You can do this! You can do this!" Body
trembling, I lost control,

Calling out Ron's name, needing protection from
yet another storm. Will I ever again be safe enough
to crawl from this hole?

He wrapped his arms around me, saying it was
okay. Heart beating fast then to a slow methodical
beat,

How did I get back to losing battle after battle?
Still, something deep inside of me refuses to accept
this defeat.

Today is another day, that God has given me, to
remember where I was once strong,

Another chance to hold on to what is right, and let go of what went wrong.

Yes, there was Another Storm Last Night but I'm still here . . .

## BLACK WATERS

Blue waters rising to the sun, turned black with the
bodies that were left dying.

Where was FEMA?

Didn't they hear us crying?

Black Waters rising to the moon, turned red with
the blood of my people, while they sit in their office
hoping this, their pencils could erase,

Yellow waters rising to the world, showing that they
knew what was happening to us, but didn't know they
would be shown face after face after face after face.

Maybe I'm just being Phyllisophical but why wouldn't
it occur to those in charge of Federal Emergency
Management Assistance to help those in dire need?

Maybe, just maybe, the hearts that are or were in those
dying bodies gasping for air, their hearts had to bleed.

Just maybe.

Those Black Waters will forever haunt my mind, as
they do my sleep and my "used-to-be sweet dreams."

Those Black Waters search for the floodgates that will eventually open to let out all of my infinite screams.

I have cried. I have bled. I have opened my soul to those who care to let the world know our pain,

And yet it still comes in the night, in the day. With the sunshine and its rainbows that I used to love so much and now I am afraid of the rain.

Black Water, Black Water, please go away, and come back another day.

Black Water, Black Water, I saw you that night asking me to come in and take a dive.

It was not my time to go. It was not my way to go. It was what God Almighty told me: "This is your time, my purpose for you to stay alive."

The Black Waters took away. And they gave. They gave some hope and others a path to a better life than "this."

The Black Waters are in my blood now, washing away what my soul needed and some I will forever miss.

## COLORING BOOKS AND JACKS

My coloring book helps me on days like this,

I open my arms to the child in me and help with what I miss.

I play jacks on the kitchen, living, dining room floor,

Because in a FEMA trailer, space is no more.

Anger, tears, emotional rip currents pull me down, up, in, and out,

All I want to do is color in my book, no, I want to shout.

Embrace the feelings. And this too shall pass.

Healing. That's what I want. And fast.

The jacks make me laugh. Especially when I "miss,"

Simpler times, a first love's kiss.

Coloring books and jacks, give me the freedom, the will.

Coloring books and jacks, my own "mental health pill."

## DREAMSICLE

Orange and White summer treat. We used to run
after the ice cream truck when we heard the bell
ringing.

We'd walk away happy, laughing, jumping up and
down, but best of all we would be singing.

Somebody's mama would always have the water hose
on, giving out free showers, washing off the sticky kids
having fun,

Sitting on the porch afterwards, watching the cars pass
by while the game played was "That's My Car," no
cares in the world or of the world, just soaking up the
sun.

Dreamsicles were my number one, all-time, favorite ice
cream treat. I was a dreamer at a very young age and
all my dreams were of love, happiness and joy to come,
Orange and White.

The helicopter that made me run for the sound that
wasn't a bell ringing: it came, it looked, it left, with
no one.

Orange and White. Sounds. Sounds of helicopters in
the night. Water lapping at the building below us,
a woman in the near distance calling for help till we
heard none.

You never know just how important being a child is
until you grow up and real life either strokes your face
softly or smacks your face hard.

This is why I hold on to some of my childlike
treasures, so that when life does hit hard and deals me
a bad hand I know which to hold on to and which to
discard.

So, I fell apart during Hurricane Katrina, it wasn't the
first time and I'm sure it won't be the last,

At least when the next slap in life comes to me I will
remember to make a better choice by not forgetting
the past.

Thank you Dreamsicle for bringing to my life, then
and now, what I needed most and that was laughter,
singing, and just joyful freedom,

Thanks to the Orange and White that came and left us,
we rescued ourselves out of there, we didn't need 'em!

## HIS ARMS

Don't cry, momma I'm okay. I know you miss me and
you cry, but I'm okay cause I'm in His Arms.

Your head is down and you can't seem to let me go and
wondering what if or maybe, but don't momma, 'cause
just like to you, I'm His baby.

There is no pain here. No hurt. Smiles are endless and
the sun it shines all the time, and like it felt in your
arms, warm.

So, don't worry about me momma, I'm okay.
You have to forgive those you feel hurt me and let
me die,

Nobody can change what has already happened; I
already know the answer to your questions of why.

Give to others the love you gave to me, and your heart
will begin to mend,

By doing this, momma, our hearts are connected and
I will feel the love you send.

His Arms, momma, feel just like yours, but I was His
from the beginning and until the end.

Right now, I'm playing in a garden with pretty flowers, and butterflies fly by or sit on my finger just to make me smile,

Don't worry momma, I'm in His Arms and though it may seem a long time to you, I'll see you again in a little while.

One more thing, momma I want you to know

Whenever something makes you smile or laugh, that's me bringing you hugs and kisses,

So, keep looking for these two things that keep us together to remove all of those tears of misses.

For us there is no good-bye. On the day that God brings you from there to here we will always be as one,

All that you have to understand, momma, is that His Will Be Done.

I'm okay momma, I'm in His Arms . . . and they feel just like yours.

Love, Your Baby Girl.

## NO SMOKING ANGEL

Dominique Jewel Santiago is an angel that tried 2 save the air I breathe

She did not give up, she is the voice of what I tried 2 conceive,

Yet and still, she understood at such a young age, what she was trying,

Day after day after day, she advocated my living, 2 keep me from dying.

Sweet face and smile, speaking perfect English and good schooling,

As much as I tried 2 get away with lies, she I was not fooling,

Reminding me of a gnat that just won't go away, all she was doing,

Was trying 2 give me life, and at it another day.

I would not give it up, not for her or another who said they cared,

Not knowing my limits or my accomplishments, I was not 2 be dared.

Thank you No Smoking Angel you tried your best,

I'm not the candidate who was willing, but the baby bird not ready 2 leave the nest.

If I die from smoking it's not your fault, because you tried 2 save by giving,

Your love was the best I ever had, and had I listened, I'd be living.

Guess what? The Lord above has a different plan for my life of "here,"

We all don't know what or how we will go, I just thank you for being such a dear.

Thank you for caring enough 2 want to save me, but some things have the say,

God has a different time, a different path for us; it ends up being His way.

## STORMY MONDAY

Last night they said we'd only get 10 percent chance of rain,

Well, it was a severe thunderstorm and again I felt "Katrina Pain."

Trying to control my state of being and the rate of my heart,

Arms closed around me, calming my fears and no more being pulled apart.

You were there when I needed you the most and life became fair,

My world calmed and the waters became dry as you slowly stroked my hair.

Stormy Monday turned into the rain I used to love, the kind that makes you sigh,

The kind where you no longer wonder about love 'cause you know it's not a lie.

Light in the darkness came to show me what tomorrow might turn out to be,

Love that I've been wanting came with it, and I felt it all belonged to me.

Goodbye, Stormy Monday, you gave to me more than you took away,

Inside of this tin can we are living in, I'm still looking forward to a better day.

Goodbye, Stormy Monday, I'm alive and I still have Lisa, Cheryl, Catherine, and Gina.

Your big sister may have scarred and hurt me, but I am healing from her, talking 'bout that damn Katrina.

Today is a good day, it's Nicholas's birthday, you know, he's ten, bright and oh so bold,

He makes a bad day good and loving my nephew is worth more than gold.

Third good-bye, Good-bye, Stormy Monday. And this too shall pass. I know.

Hello, today and tomorrow, if it is His Will, I will for a long, long time continue to grow.

## THE STORM IS OVER

Nicholas: Mommy, the wind is blowing very strongly, I'm afraid.

Mother: It's okay Nicholas, why don't we get supplies to help us prepare.

What are supplies, Mommy?

Supplies are things like: a flashlight, candles, food, batteries, and water.

Why do we need those things, Mommy?

We need a flashlight just in case our lights go out, then we will be able to see if it gets dark. We need batteries because they make the flashlight work. See?

We need candles so that we have light to see in different places in the house. See? Only adults can light candles. We need food so we can have snacks and something to eat while the storm passes us by. And we need water to drink when we get thirsty.

Mommy, I am still afraid. Will the storm hurt us?

No, the storm will not hurt us because we are prepared and we helped each other to be safe.

How long will the storm last, Mommy?

I don't know for sure, but it won't be a long time and before you know it, the storm will be over.

Mommy, I feel safer because we have the things that we need until the storm is over.

Yes, Nicholas. That's what mommies do when there is a storm. She takes care of her baby that she loves—and look, now the storm is over and you were very brave.

Thank you Mommy, you made everything better because you love me and I love you, yeaaaaah, and the storms are over! Mommy, can we play a game now?

Sure, honey. What game would you like to play?

I want to play Storm Chaser.

And why do you want to play that game, Nicholas?

Because we chased the storm away together and I'm not afraid anymore. I love you, Mommy.

## THE WINDOW AND THE LADY IN BLACK

Hearing her voice, I could not help but want to hear,

So I kept running to the window if for nothing else, out of pure fear.

Flashlight shining on her, I could not see,

So I called out: where are you? Where are you? She said nothing.

All night I wondered how far the water had risen on her. I could not sleep.

How could I leave my family, wade in those dark waters, with my sanity to keep?

Dozing off time to time, fanning Ron in the heat, and afraid to close my eyes,

What if she can be saved? What if I waited too long and she actually dies?

Faint sounds of "Help. Help me." She never answered me back and I lost hope,

I wonder to this day if she got out. I wonder if she survived when nobody threw the rope.

Why didn't I go out and try to help her? Who left her there and why was I the only voice?

I was falling apart, and my mind was not in the path of any reasonable choice.

So, I left her moaning. I left her looking for someone to raise his or her hand,

I want her to know what I had left was not enough to make a stand.

I'm sorry I didn't look for her to pull her out of where she stood,

Had I had the strength to go forward, I would.

To the lady in darkness who I could hear but could not see,

Please forgive me for not coming, I was not who I am, I was not me.

## THOUGHTS OF SUICIDE

Deafening wind blowing in my ears. Darkness falls
and day is no more, while we wait for Katrina to come
ashore.

Walls begin to fall down around us. Fear is pumping
the blood to and through my heart; the noise from
inside is when pieces begin falling apart.

Wondering now, will we live or die? Do I laugh or do I
cry? Should I frown? Will we drown?

Heart rate will not come down. Drink stolen whiskey,
it helps for a minute or two. That didn't help, now
what will I do?

Oh, but wait. That old slave spirit came up inside
of me and pushed me to up. They said "Don't you
dare!"

A dead body is a dead body. You still breathe and that
is the only thing you need, all you need is to care.

For all that you had, that was placed on your heart
and mind, there is a God above and for you He has
a plan.

He placed you here for a purpose, for a reason. What happened to you and the others was already written, it was the time, and it was the season.

In the same way, those responsible for the wrongful suffering will on Judgment Day have to give their reason.

I'm here today, giving all the glory to God, blessed with another season.

## TODAY IS A GOOD DAY

Simply because I awoke this morning with the peaceful feeling that God loves me.

And no matter what goes on in this world my goal is for Him, you see?

As I spoke my love for Him and the strong desire to please,

Worry and dismay slowly began to ease.

Those who hurt me and those whom I have hurt are forgiven and are asked to forgive.

Anger is no longer, and resolution is for what I live.

A stumble here, a trip and fall there, perfection is a thing of the past,

Judgment and hate are not mine, only love to last.

The story has been told and with it go the memories of hurt and pain,

My search is for the sun to warm my heart and the comfort of the rain.

## USED 2 B

After the tears, after Hurricane Katrina, there were no more,

I waited and wanted for them to come, like Katrina, ashore.

They never did, so I pushed them out with drink after drink,

Realizing this thing was deeper than I thought, or would think.

Then the pills to sleep kept away the dreams, those drowning dreams,

Night after night after night they'd creep in until my heart burst at the seams.

Stop it! Stop it! I didn't drown! I didn't die! I'm still here! I did survive!

Why? Why was it so hard to believe that I was after all, still alive?

Used 2 B I'd sit and wonder if this were the real world and I was just lost,

Questioning whether I wanted to stay sane but at what cost.

Used 2 B I wanted to ball up into a knot and crawl in the black hole,

That black hole of no hopes, no belief, and no trust: was I losing my soul?

Then sister, G. let someone know that I had a story to tell,

The crew of 40 Acres and a Mule threw me a lifeline, a lifeline out of hell.

I began to feel cared about, loved and needed. I began to once again to feel me!

Now, Used 2 B doesn't live here, thanks to Jesus, the crew of 40, a Mule, and my hero . . . Mr. Spike Lee!

## WOULD YOU HAVE COME IF I DROWNED?

*To my daddy, Phillip Montana*

Would you have come if I'd drowned, daddy? Maybe?
Maybe Not?

What if they'd shown me in water screaming your
name?

Or how 'bout this: What if they'd shown my body
wasted to rot?

Would you have come then? Would you come to see
your child's face?

Or would it be the way it's always been: me in your
heart not having a place?

So many times, while I was hungry, thirsty, and
fighting to stay alive,

I tried to picture your face from the picture I lost
in the storm, strangely enough, seeing you one day
helped me to survive.

See, I feel very strongly about us meeting one day.

Phillip and Phyllis will meet, either here or there,

Either way, my heart knows that it will be too much for you and me to bear.

But it will be done, by the grace of God, it should be done, because you do not know who it is that I was, am, and am going to be.

Would you come if I said: I Love you and it doesn't matter what happened between you and my mother?

Would you come if I said that I needed you, I forgive you and I want for my father, no other?

Well, I do. Forgive you. Need you. Love you. If you never come it's okay.

Maybe in our next life in heaven . . . Maybe one day.

# ACKNOWLEDGMENTS AND THANKS

First, I would like to thank Mr. Spike Lee for the inspiration and "push" to write this story. If it weren't for you, this book would not be. You are now, officially, family.

I want to thank the following people: Ms. Erin Malone and Ms. Jennifer Rudolph-Walsh at William Morris Agency for their super support and guidance; Erin, you are one in a million!

Ms. Malaika Adero with Simon & Schuster, Inc., and Atria Books for the lessons and inspiration to want and get more from life.

My mother, Mrs. Clovina Rita McCoy, for always being there for me and having our "arguments." My sisters, who are the best in the world. I could not live without y'all. Catherine Montana-Gordon, my every day all-day counselor at heart, you love me like Stevie Nicks and you saved my life. Cheryl Ann Montana, my "Hurricane Katrina Storm

Tracker" in Los Angeles; thanks for helping save our lives, and may your beauty salon, SASSY (Serious About Service Spoil Yourself) prosper greater than you know. Lisa Ann Montana, my "Brooklyn Tranquility." We are twins born on different dates. My brother, Thomas W. McCoy, you already know that growing is the best part of life. And to my late brother-in-law, Mr. Helmon Michael Gordon Jr., you will always inspire me to be the best no matter what. I miss you like yesterday, man. To my nephews, Nicholas Tyler Gordon, Kaleb Joseph Bell; and my nieces, Jahia Rita Montana Forbes, Alesia McCoy, Indya McCoy, and Teelah McCoy: I love all of you. My two sweet potato pie aunts, Mrs. Augusta Kendrick and Ms. Jean Frank, thank you for sharing God's Word. My aunt Marion Kendrick, come out of the past and live the life that God gave to you. To my favorite uncle, Mr. James Frank Jr., you are my hero and you know what I mean. My cousin Mr. Kim Santiago and his wife Ainka, thanks for being there and bringing back your income tax company, Max Tax, to the city.

My "No Smoking Angel," Dominique Jewel Santiago, thank you for all of your spell checks; your future is bright and promising, keep on making the "A's." My cousin-in-law Denean Santiago, for keeping it real. To my loving and supportive cousins Eugene, Emmitt, and John Henry Kendrick; Nicole Kendrick; Tamara Kendrick; Deionna Frank; Mr. Keefe Frank; and Mr. Stan "The Man" Taylor, one of the smartest brothers I ever met.

The *Times-Picayune* newspaper for "telling it like it is."

Mrs. Marcia Tureaud and Mr. Mark Tureaud, for their hospitality and open arms.

Warner and Katie Leblanc for their love and support. Mrs. Leslie Byrd, my Washington, D.C., friend, see you soon. Ms. LaShawn Watson, the "diva with a loving heart." Ms. Lorraine "Jah" Latchman, Brooklyn Love, my friend. Mr. Larry Smith, my knight in shining armor. My aunts Marion Donelly, Wilma Owens, Delores Mills, and June Thompson, thanks for your love and support. Ms. Kim Parsley, Autistic Life Skills Teacher at Pine Forest Elementary School in Humble, Texas. Ms. Thelma Clardy, attorney, in Dallas. Mr. Fred Johnson, who is a true man for the people. Thanks for your knowledge. Mr. Graylen Banks, keep it talking, I'll keep learning.

Everyone at 40 Acres & A Mule Filmworks, you are the best, thanks for the love.

Mr. and Mrs. Melvin (Judy) Hills for the room in the city. Ms. Brenda Valteau for all your love and support.

A special dedication of love to my late cousin, Yellow Pocahontas Chief Allison "Tootie" Montana, I miss you dearly. Mrs. Joyce Montana, Daryl and Sabrina Montana. The entire Montana family. My dear friend, national guard sergeant Morris Patterson, thank you for keeping our city safer.

Ms. Sue Perez with the Red Cross, keep helping us, you're the greatest!

Ms. Dawanda "Tee" Davis and family, strong inspirations in this family. Thank you to author Toni Morrison for saying to me, "I know you." Meeting you changed my life!

To the entire response teams that helped rescue our city during Hurricane Katrina: Louisiana National Guard, U.S. Coast Guard, New Orleans Police Department, New Orleans

Fire Department, and all other volunteers and caring hearts, thank you!

To the staff at Kelly Air Force base in San Antonio, I'll never forget your kind treatment.

Ms. Sheila Nevins at HBO Films and Documentaries, thank you for your kind words and for caring enough to bring our time of need to the world.

To the Corps of Engineers Agency: Fix the damn levees!

Thanks to Bishop T.D. Jakes for inspiring me to reposition my life. I won't be cussing forever. Thanks to all of the spiritual leaders, talk show hosts, actors, and actresses who showed us during Hurricane Katrina the difference between acting and the real deal.

Many thanks to all of those who returned home and are trying to redevelop their lives.

And to those who are trying but can't come back, please keep trying and don't give up.

Ms. Judy Aley, Sam Pollard, and Butch Robinson were the first to interview me for *When the Levees Broke* and began the saving of lives in New Orleans, I will never forget you guys!

Mrs. Rhonshá "Shay" Bryant, my best friend in the world. Ms. Shay, you are so intelligent and caring, life is going to give you so much back, you just wait and see.

Mrs. Shera Burell-Young and Steve Young, thanks for letting me run to your home for shelter when those damn storms came while I was still living in the FEMA trailer, and my two "nephews," Steve Jr. and Kendrick Young.

Mr. Albert Cordell Thomas (C-Lo of the Uptown Rulers), "won't kneel, won't bow."

Ms. Michelle, "Me'Key" McWilliams, the songbird the world will hear one day and kick itself for not hearing her sooner.

Mr. Vernon Smith, you have a heart of gold and we are blessed to know you. Thanks for all of your help down in San Antonio.

My family at NOLA Animal Clinic in New Orleans East—Dr. Lily Rai, Ms. Judy, Ayanna, and all of the technicians there who helped me so lovingly with my puppy, Mr. Brooklyn Montana-Leblanc. You guys are the absolute best.

Dr. Sarah Fernandez at Oschner Hospital, who should have her own talk show on how to care for others, and her assistant, Tanisha (didn't I ask you to tell me how to spell your name!). Thank you for helping me to heal. Dr. Kristi Soileau, who helped me to smile more by fixing the mouth that will speak to the world now and in the future. Dr. Phillips at CBD Dental who, with great patience, made my smile prettier than before.

Thank you, Tonette Harrison, for doing my "do" like nobody else in "the east," and the ladies at Gayle Laurance Ltd.—Lisa T. Mountain and Michele LeVasseur—for keeping it real all the time! To my cousins Larry Hayes, Lil Cleon, Hope Frank, and Madeline.

Ms. Cozeth M. Blackwell and her daughter, Lisa, two of the most caring people I never even met but showed me big love!

Ms. Ducre at City Hall, I could never forget you!

Father Tony who married Ron and me at St. Jude Church. And my "English Muffin," Suzette of "Suzette Art

Couture," your hats are a true creation from a true heart.

I can't forget my motivational cousin, Mr. Joseph "Joe" Frank; thanks for opening my eyes to the Bohemian Spillway and the land of our people, we ain't done yet! And my cousin Sam Fowler, for looking out for me on the Sandy Cove block, thanks a million!

To all of the people in New Orleans who have come up to me and hugged and kissed and shaken my hand for speaking out, I thank you from the bottom of my heart; you are all truly and honestly my strength to keep on keeping on.

Ms. Arlene Craft over at Big Chief Laundry, you are my girl!

Ms. Crystal B. Harris over at Unlimited Stylez & Kutz Barber and Beauty Salon, we need more people like you in the world.

Mrs. Tonya Lewis Lee, thank you sooooo much for "Please, Puppy Please"; you, Spike, and Kadir Nelson did an excellent job! I loved it and read it over and over and over again!

Ms. Akisa, my sister-in-law, thanks for letting me "act a fool."

The security department at the W Hotel in New York, y'all are my family, and I love you all!

I know he can't read it, but my puppy, Brooklyn, is my lifesaver, he brings me so much joy and helps to heal my heart from the storm of storms.

Last, but damn sure not least, I want to thank my husband, Ron A. Leblanc Sr., you are the best man I'll ever know. Thank you for holding me up when I just wanted to lie down and die. Your love is all I need. I loved you before

I met you. We were meant to be together, and like my sister Cheryl says, "TRUST AND BELIEVE THAT!"

And just like living in New Orleans is like breathing for life, anyone who I did not mention, you are in my heart, and you know that! This love is real y'all! Peace. Mrs. Phyllis Montana-Leblanc.

Printed in the United States
By Bookmasters